... the most highly acclaimed...
heart warmer of the season...

... funny, inspiring , full of hope and love...
... a "life changer" for "kids from 9 to 90"

... perfect for today's times...

"Your book touched my heart." GP

"No longer am I a SCUM BAG. I am free. I am a child of God. . I am somebody". The words in your book have changed my life forever." PM

"It's only the second book I've ever read cover to cover IN MY LIFE!" MB

"Your book helps me keep going-one day at a time. I read a few pages of your book every night before dozing off. Thank you for being an inspiration in my life." LT

"I got your book at the signing last night-one of my best friends is in the battle of his life. Please sign a copy for him-I'm going to make a special trip to see him this afternoon." JH

"What a wonderful book! You are one of a kind and amazing. Your insight to God's love and promises. Keep up the strong faith and Believe." JS

"Your book touched my heart and soul, as well as my funny bone. Thank you for sharing." VP

DREAM BIG

NEVER

GIVE UP

By Butch Peelle

Wilmington, Ohio's #1 Realtor for the past 26 years

Update since First Printed Edition

Valentine's Day 2011

Nobody could be better qualified than Butch Peelle to write on the subject of determination and personal courage in the face of adversity.

'Everyday, Expect a Miracle' was first published in October 2009, a very adverse time for the people of Wilmington, Ohio.

The sudden and dramatic loss of 8,000 jobs from southern Ohio in 2008 foreshadowed the general downturn in the American economy as a whole. Wilmington became known as the 'epicenter of the great recession'.

Butch Peelle put pen to paper as a means of uplifting the spirits of his friends, neighbors, and community. Knowing that a person, community or nation with high spirits will embrace hope and that in a spirited people there is no room for despair.

In this second edition of the 'little book', Butch Peelle offers an equally uplifting message. He draws upon his roots, a gusty never say die Quaker, and compels America to claw its way back to the top - one day at a time. Butch Peelle reminds us of our basic principles and that we are a resilient, proud, and hard working faithful people who 'Everyday, Expect a Miracle'.

Eric LaMont Gregory

TABLE OF CONTENTS

Foreward

Butch Peelle and I have something very much in common. Butch and I both had mothers whose peace, whose nurturing, whose loyalty and whose glow from their faces were brighter than the noon sun on Pebble Beach. From modest beginnings, Butch Peelle shows how anyone can, through deep faith, persistence, guts and a NEVER GIVE UP ATTITUDE can have a better life, can have brighter days, more peace filled nights and stress-free months within your soul throughout your years. You will find this faith-based lifestyle which Butch Peelle has traveled over the past twenty five years to be an exciting journey.

As you turn the pages of this little book, you will find it to be more than just a book!

I believe you should take out your yellow legal pad, your pen or pencil and take notes while you journey through these areas of faith, angels and miracles.

I, like Butch, believe that LIFE IS A JOURNEY, NOT A DESTINATION!

So let's tee it up and get started!!

Greg Nared

I dedicate this little book to Almighty God, without whose miracles, the existence of my LIFE would never have been; the footprints He set forth for the path of my life which were occurring before I was even aware and the absolute beautiful LIFE which He has permitted me to enjoy.

This little book would never have been possible if it were not for Dollie, "the brown-eyed girl", who married me so many years ago and my two beautiful daughters, Tracey and Carrie; what can I say but thank you and that I love you more than you will ever know.

Also, I dedicate this little book to every student who was at the Wilmington Junior High School from 1969-1974 (making up the WHS Graduating Classes of 1974-1978). These students, during their seventh and eighth grade years, will never know how they touched me then; and the pride I have had as they have grown into adults, raising great kids; serving as community leaders in government, business and the medical profession.

In addition, I dedicate this little book to every person whom I ever had the privilege and pleasure of serving in a real estate relationship.

Furthermore, I dedicate this little book to anyone who has ever had a "down" day.

And, finally, I dedicate this little book to anyone who wants more peace, more love and a greater life than where they're at now.

SECTION I

Butch's Story

THANK YOU...

for reading this little book.

It can have a profound change in your life!

IF YOU WANT IT TO!

Love,

Butch

Introduction

"It's not where you start; it's not even where you finish; it's the light and the love that you put in other people's faces each and every day while you travel this journey called LIFE" ~Butch Peelle

You're what you are, you're where you are, because of what's gone into your mind; you can change what you are, you can change where you are by changing what goes into your mind!!

As a flaming optimist, I'm the kind of guy who would row out to capture Moby Dick and take the tartar sauce with me!

I'm the kind of guy that sees a glass half full even if there are only a couple dribbles left in the bottom of the glass.

But it hasn't always been that way.

• •

Having been reared the son of a dirt farmer in southern Ohio, there were times when I was in elementary and junior high school when I would just hurt deep inside. My self worth, the value of my life, during those times, would today be termed "low self esteem." If you've ever had these feelings, you will see, as you turn the pages of this book, *how you can lift yourself up, how every day can be a brand new opportunity for you!*

Four years ago, my friend Bruce McKee said, "You know, you really ought to write a book!" I said, "You really ought to stop smoking whatever it is you've been smoking!"

I went on to say "Bruce, who in the world would have any interest in what I would have to say?" He answered, "You'd be surprised; people just wonder what you're thinking; many people would like to know your thoughts and the reasons why you have been so successful."

A year later, Bruce inquired "have you given any more thought to writing that book?"

I said "Bruce, I love you, but no one would really care!" Finally, I said "Bruce, you go home and you come back in with ten titles of chapters for this book and a list of things you think people would have an interest in, then that will give me a place to start." He returned with 46 topics that he and his wife Vanessa had come up with that weekend.

It took another two years of them patiently waiting for me to begin the book, but on the onset of our nation's devastating recession in 2008, which hit particularly hard in our small community of Wilmington, Ohio, it finally seemed to be the right time to sit down and write "the book".

Many people don't realize that "The Recession" hit the real estate industry in many areas of the country towards the end of 2006. By the beginning of 2007 we recognized that we were not just in a slump but a major crisis. We were very deep in debt and there was no way to make the payments. Our rental properties were now costing more than they were bringing in. Over thirty percent of our renters were unable to make payments. We were on a sinking ship, and it had a hole bigger than the Titanic's.

Thus, the task was before me. I had to go back to the beginning and dig out of a desperate situation. I had done it before, but it appeared that this situation had the potential to be worse than any I had encountered in the past.

So, I decided to write this book to encourage myself, and anyone else out there that is climbing up out of a big hole.

Expect a Miracle!

■■

Think you're a scum bag?

Think you're worthless?

Many of us have at one time or

another!

HIS EYE IS ON THE SPARROW SO I KNOW HE'S WATCHING ME

I was born in a little house outside of Martinsville, a small village in Clinton County, Ohio just a few miles south from the city of Wilmington.

The snow and the blizzard conditions on that cold January day were not enough to keep Dr. Fullerton from making the house call to assist my mother in her delivery.

The make shift bed in front of the coal burning stove in the living room, was primitive at best; apparently, it was a very painstaking and difficult delivery for my mother.

Though we didn't talk about it often, my mother did eventually tell me that at the time of my birth, I was a blue baby (presumed to be <u>dead</u> <u>on</u> <u>arrival</u>).

Dr. Fullerton, believing I was beyond help, laid me on the foot of the bed to work diligently to save the life of my mother, who had hemorrhaged in a horrific way.

While the country doctor was working on my mother, my grandmother, Carrie Lundy, gently picked me up, softly whispered a prayer, as she massaged me and gave me a swat on my bottom.

I then let out a loud YELP!

Even though I was not aware at that time, it is very obvious to me today, that God's angels were surrounding my mother, my grandmother Lundy and me.

The saving of my little body, giving me the opportunity to enjoy LIFE, was the first of hundreds of MIRACLES which my Heavenly Father would provide for this unworthy, undeserving human being.

After me came my brothers, Bill and Bob...

∙∙∙

WE ARE FAMILY

When I was five years old, we moved from Martinsville to a small farm near Mowrystown, Ohio, another small village in neighboring Highland County. My father eked out a living on a little 96 acre farm on Taylorsville Road. We lived back a long lane in an old 1 ½ story house; I was down there not too long ago- at that time, they were using the old house to store seedcorn and fertilizer- however, they won't be using it for that *very much longer*... it's just about had it!

Now, I don't want you to misunderstand me; I don't want you to think that when I was a little kid that we didn't have plenty to eat at our house! I know we had plenty because every night at supper when I'd pass my plate around for seconds, they'd always tell me, they'd say "Nope, you've had plenty!" So, I <u>know</u> <u>we</u> <u>had</u> <u>plenty</u>!!

As you now know, there were three kids in my family; I had two brothers; we all slept in one bed. I *didn't sleep alone until I got married!*

When I was a kid, central heat meant you had either a wood-burning stove or, if you were more fortunate, you had an upper-scale Ziglar oil space heater in the middle of the room; we had the wood-burning stove.

I was thirteen before I knew my name wasn't "Get Wood"!

I guess it was a good thing that we were isolated from a lot of thigs. It kept me from getting into more trouble than I already had. Later in life I began speaking quite often to high school students. I'd hear a lot about "a pot and a trip". I told 'em "when I was a kid, we put a pot underneath the bed so <u>we</u> <u>wouldn't</u> <u>have</u> <u>to</u> <u>make</u> <u>the</u> <u>trip</u> (to the outhouse, that is)!"

• •

LITTLE THINGS

One morning, I must have been around 6, my mom was wearing a necklace with something very small at the bottom of it. I was struck by how very miniscule it was so I asked her about it. "Oh" she said, "Butch, it's a grain of mustard seed." I said "well, Mommy, it's awful small." She explained "Honey, the Bible says that if you have just as much faith as this little tiny grain of mustard seed, you can move mountains! <u>Nothing</u> <u>is</u> <u>impossible</u> or <u>ever</u> <u>will</u> <u>be</u> <u>impossible</u> <u>if</u> <u>you</u> <u>have</u> <u>FAITH</u>!"

To be sure I understood, she continued, "Butch, what that means is that Faith in God is the most important attribute that you will ever need. And with Faith, through the direction of Almighty God, you *can do* and *become anything* and <u>everything</u> in which you *set your mind and heart to do*."

<u>I</u> <u>never</u> <u>forgot</u> <u>that</u>!

• •

PEOPLE GOT TO BE FREE

My Mother had two books that could always be easily found at our house: The Holy Bible and a Sears Roebuck catalog!

And she would say, "Now this one's <u>where</u> <u>you're</u> <u>going</u> (as she held up the Bible) and then she'd say "this one will help you <u>enjoy</u> <u>the</u> <u>trip</u>. This one's your 'religious belief' and this one's your 'pick and choose'."

But she'd say, "Don't get the two confused! For you see, it's these two books that make America great; the <u>free</u> <u>enterprise</u> <u>system</u> on the one hand and our <u>deep</u> <u>seeded</u> <u>faith</u> on the other."

Many times she would add, "<u>I</u> <u>know</u> <u>not</u> <u>what</u> <u>tomorrow</u> <u>holds</u>, <u>but</u> <u>I</u> <u>know</u> <u>who</u> <u>holds</u> <u>tomorrow</u>."

- -

LOVE IS ALL AROUND

The one Christmas I remember in Mowrystown, I was 9, Billy was 6 and Bobby was 4. It was Christmas time and for us young kids, the last ten days before Christmas seemed like a year. This particular Christmas, the three of us boys received a gift we were to share.

The gift had been provided by our Grandmother May Peelle. Somehow, she had found a way to purchase four eight-foot long 2 x 4 boards. Each of the 2 x 4's had been cut into eight inch links with a fourth of the eight inch blocks red, a fourth blue, a fourth green and a fourth yellow. With the exception of a hand full of trinkets, that was our Christmas.

I kind of looked at Bill and he kind of looked at me; Bob was just happy to know it was Christmas and wasn't really old enough to be able to comprehend this magnificent treasure of forty-eight *eight inch blocks*!

Being the brave one I asked Dad and Mom what we were to do with these blocks. "Oh," they said "you'll use them to build things." The only thing that Bill and I could figure out was it was a step above playing in the mud holes in the backyard like the past summer.

However, our confusion didn't last long- we started building things with the blocks and had a wonderful Christmas dinner which Mom prepared. Just having the love and warmth of our Mother at home with us for the day was Christmas enough!

But over the next few months, did we ever build things!!

BOBBY

The following Christmas, after the 48 assorted colorful building blocks, for the first time, one of us boys got a NEW toy. My brother Bob, who had just turned 5, received a very cool miniature cast iron bright red International Farmall toy tractor. Just months before, my Father had arranged to have about twenty feet of a concrete sidewalk poured between our graveled driveway and the back door of our back-the-lane Mowrystown house.

When the weather cleared up, Bob would drive that little tractor as fast as he could to one end of the sidewalk, flip it around, and then drive toward the other end at *full speed*. During the next few months, he must have put 50,000 miles on that little red Farmall tractor!

When Bob was in the second grade, he came home one evening after school and couldn't find his little red tractor. So at supper time, he tearfully asked if anyone had seen it.

My Father announced that he had given that little red tractor away to a "poor family" down the road.

Years later, recalling this devastating discovery, Bob retorted, "at the time, I didn't think there was any family poorer than we were!"

. . . .

DON'T MESS WITH BILL

When I was, maybe, eight, one Sunday early afternoon, my father (known to many as Hubie) and I were in the living room (he was wearing his usual Clark Gable undershirt-reading the paper).

Suddenly, my brother Bill was knocking profusely at the back door (he must have been five) yelling "Daddy! Daddy! Daddy! Come here Daddy, come here Daddy!"

Well, Dad didn't seem to get too rattled when any of his three boys tried to scream out for his attention. However, Billy did get my curiosity, so I decided to go out the screen door to see what he was up to.

Billy said, "Come here man." So I dutifully followed him.

On the rear of the trunk of Dad's 1949 white two door Chevrolet coupe, my brother Billy, with his knife, just below the Chevrolet insigne had carved the letters, B I L L Y.

I said, "Wow, Billy that's pretty good!" Inside me, however, I was smiling my face off because I knew Billy was about to really get his brains beat in by our Dad! I knew what I would have gotten if I had done that, so Billy was in for the beating of a lifetime.

Finally, Billy *did* get Hubie's attention. I was so pumped!

I had never seen a five year old about to get completely pulverized. As a brother, it was always cool to have the heat on him instead of me. For some reason, as the devilish imp I was, I could not wait to see Dad go completely berserk!

Billy finally got dad out of his favorite chair, pulled him through the rear storm door and down the twenty feet of brother Bob's favorite tractor path; Dad lumbered over toward the automobile with Bill encouraging him every step of the way.

Billy pointed out his artistic pride and joy on the rear of the trunk.

Dad's veins around his neck began to get somewhere near the color of grape kool-aid; his veins were starting to show that there was no anger management class in the entire world that could control his reaction!

I figured death was not an option, but it was going to be close!
As dad was about ready to take deadly action toward my younger brother, Billy looked up at him and with all the love and sincerity of a little puppy dog explained "Daddy, the next time when we're at the Highland County Fair in Hillsboro, our car won't be hard to find like it was the last time; that's why I put my name on the back of the car, daddy."

That sincere, profound announcement by my little brother was even too much for my dad; he walked slowly back toward the old house without saying a single word.

I was crushed.

GOOD VIBRATIONS

My mother and I once went over to Hillsboro to see about getting one of those new "ringer washin' machines".

The salesman was telling my mother about credit- credit was just coming in then! He said, "Now lady, all you have to do is put $10 down; then you don't pay anything for six months."

My mother looked up and shot back: *"Who told you about us?"*

∙∙∙

MACK THE KNIFE

My Mother taught us so many little vignettes about life.

On more than one occasion she would put a small brownie or piece of cake in front of my brother Bill and I. And she would say "Now Butch, you cut the cake down the center and then, Bill, you get first choice."

You can't imagine how steady my little dirty fingernail hands were in cutting the piece of cake into the two most equal pieces possible!

My Mother had a keen sense of fairness and wanted to pass that value onto her boys.

∙∙∙

Grandma Lundy, me and "ole Bob"-
(I'm the one on the right)

The Peelle boys digging!

Mowrystown Farm, an early
photo of the original Rugrats!

Bob and his little red Farmall tractor... it appears he was taking up a collection ... probably for gas money.

Boy, could Bob spin that thing around on a dime! He must have put 50,000 miles on that little tractor- amazing since he only had 20 feet of concrete to drive on!

Younger brother, Bill, playing "GO TELL IT ON THE MOUNTAIN!"

First Grade-
What a hunk of
burnin' love!

"Little Bo-Peep (Bo-Butch) has lost his sheep and doesn't know where to find them. So, like a good shepherd, Little Bo-Butch decided to take a nap."

Mowrystown farm: Butch, Bill and Bob; notice Bill's closeness to the car with his hand raised as if declaring this oath, "I promise that this little white car will never get lost again!"

OH, WHAT A NIGHT

When I was in the fourth grade lightning struck the barn late one Autumn night. The barn held a $1,000 worth of tobacco, which in those days, in the Appalachian region of southern Ohio, was a major crop.

For many farm folks, the sale of tobacco represented a major portion of their annual farm income. When the leaves had fully cured in the barn, the farmers hauled the tobacco to the auction barns in Maysville, Kentucky or some other Northern Kentucky auction house.

The lightening strike ignited a fire with flames reaching as high as the black sky. Apparently, for Dad and Mom, this was the proverbial straw that "broke the camel's back" on the little farm near Mowrystown. They were ready to go!

Within months, we moved to a farm which Dad rented near a little Norman Rockwell crossroads called Bridges, just three miles south of Leesburg, still in Highland County.

THAT'S THE WAY LOVE IS

Years later, my Mother would say that those years on the Mowrystown farm in that old 1 ½ story house were, as a family, the happiest years we ever had.

She was probably right. We were dirt poor.

As three little rug rats, we were oblivious to the financial problems our parents were having.

I will always be thankful that in those days, we didn't have the government telling us how poor we were. We didn't *know* we were poor.

At the time, we didn't even *think* we were poor.

KNOCK THREE TIMES

We boys, Billy, Bobby & I were so excited about the new farm near Leesburg!

It had four (count 'em one, two, three, four barns) on the farm; in addition, there were actually two houses- both in considerable disrepair; the living room floor of the one we lived in was like walking on a trampoline; the hand-pump in the kitchen sink was the extension of the dug well; simply working the handle would bring up water to drink or to wash dishes or whatever was needed.

To our amazement, the outhouse had three holes of various sizes, apparently, one for Daddy, Mommy, and one for a kid.

Of course, it dawned on us later that there would never be a time when three people (or even two!) would be using the oversized outhouse more than _one person at a time_!

....

WHERE COULD I GO, BUT TO THE LORD

There was a little country Quaker Church called the Hardins Creek Friends Church located about a mile from where we lived.

Our parents would always make sure that we got there on Sunday morning, even though we were expected to find our way back home after church service. Usually, we walked.

On more than one occasion a kind-hearted neighbor or church member would pick us up and drop us by the farm.

....

24

I'M ON THE OUTSIDE

When you are raised on a farm and the closest friends you have are a jersey cow, a couple of sows, a dozen or so feeder pigs and 15 to 20 chickens, there is something about your after school social life that seems missing.

My self worth was somewhere between very little and none.

In the seventh grade, I left my study hall chair to go to the library area which was on one end of the study hall (as in many schools at that time, the library was not a separate area of research but was more of an afterthought generally being a part of the study hall area).

As I was picking out a book, a pretty high school junior looked down with disdain at my dirty fingernails, then glanced over at her peers as if to say "what a scum bag this kid is!"

These sorts of encounters, coupled with my tumultuous relationship I had with my father did nothing to improve my self esteem.

∎∎

ONLY THE LONELY

Seventh grade dance...

My first dance...

Wow, how I dreaded this garbage; it was a junior high dance, which is bad enough. As a low-level seventh grader, it took all the courage and gumption in the world to ask Sue to the dance. As it got closer to the night of the affair, I learned that she was actually in love with an eighth grader.

I didn't even know what love was, but she had eyes for this older kind of a good looking fair haired guy.

My father and I arrived at her house to pick her up and Hubie drove us to the dance.

I pretended to smile as we walked into the gymnasium together. We sat in the bleacher seats; I think it was the second song when Harold came over and asked her if she would dance with him. She bolted off that bleacher seat never to return!

For the next three hours she had her lips locked on his ear like it was a Fig Newton. For the next three hours, I sat in the bleacher seat wondering when Hubie could come and pick me up! Let her find her own way home!

Eventually the wonderful event ended, someone turned the lights on and *lovergirl* walked over to me as if to say, "is my ride ready?" We got into the back seat of Hubie's car, took her back to her farm house (the interior of our car smelling like a combination of 5-10-10 fertilizer and seed corn). As I recall, she ran up the steps to her house as I was still trying to maneuver out of the rear seat.

Hubie drove me home in silence.

He must have been tremendously impressed at my manhood skills.

YOU KEEP ME HANGIN' ON

When I was fifteen, I was with my mom in the little farm kitchen at Leesburg, I mentioned to her that I would like to go to college.

She responded "Honey, you don't understand."

Well, I did understand! We had <u>no</u> <u>money</u>!

So, for my Mother, who had more faith than anyone I knew, and even though I knew what she said was true, to say this, it was still a tough blow.

Now in those days Oscar Robertson was my hero! For those too young to remember, Oscar Robertson was the Michael Jordan, the LeBron James of his day!! The night he scored 56 points against St. Johns at Madison Square Gardens was college news throughout the country!

This lanky 6'5 guard was the talk of the nation!

My Uncle Chic and Uncle Homer would sit around the kitchen table raving about Oscar; each tale became more embellished than the last!

Sometime, after having a conversation with my Mom, I was reading an article about Oscar; I happened to notice in a side bar how the University of Cincinnati offered a co-op or work-study program where a student could go to school for three months and work for three months.

I thought, wow, maybe I could do that.

....

HAVE FUN IN THE SUMMERTIME

During my freshman year at Leesburg, my parents announced that we were going to be moving to Martinsville.

That was the most devastating news I had heard since Dad gave Bob's tractor away!

The only two kids I knew that went to Martinsville School were Nancy and David Custis. They lived down the lane right next to my Grandma Peelle, whose farm we were going to be moving to.

My brothers and I played baseball over the summers with David and Nancy (who was a tomboy and a pretty good athlete).

Nonetheless, I certainly didn't want to leave Leesburg!

As a freshman, I was just getting really good at running the alleys with my town buddies, learning how to do really obnoxious things. I was on the verge of becoming dumb and dumber.

We pulled some pretty cool stunts, including tipping over an outhouse with a fellow who was apparently doing more than just reading "The Sears-Roebuck catalog."

He came after us yelling and screaming words that I had not had the privilege of hearing before.

Thank God I found a tree to hide behind while my buddies continued to run for their lives!

With all this camaraderie and mischief just on the threshold of becoming an art, it is no wonder I didn't want to move!

That summer- the summer of 1961- that was the <u>longest</u> summer ever.

YOU'VE GOT A FRIEND

The good news!

The trauma of moving was short lived, as it turned out.

The kids at Martinsville High School were very kind and took us under their wings. Those two years, my sophomore and junior years, which I spent at Martinsville, were two of the best years of my schooling.

I will never forget the kindness shown by Craig Zeigler, Gary Rinehart, Bill VanPelt, Roger Camp, Stevie Valentine, Curtis Couch, Jerry Soale, Marvin Summers, Mark Flora, Gordon Ledford, Bill McCandless, Steve Burroughs, Ronnie Purcell, Jerry Griffith, Elvin Shelton, Danny Watson, Jack Farquer, Howard Pinney, Dick McKinley, Eddie Roush and other great kids who welcomed us.

It was a time when I almost thought I was going to be *somebody!*

SPLISH SPLASH

On the farm, it was imposed upon each of us boys that we would take a bath in the morning prior to getting on the bus and heading for school.

Boys, being what they are, are not that crazy about water and soap being used together anyway!

This was complicated by the fact that when I was a kid (and still today) I was never an early riser. I know it's crazy; I just fight getting up in the morning just as much as I abhor going to bed at night!

Anyway, there were three years when we lived in the Martinsville house when I did make an effort to be the first one up.

Why?!

Because Hubie's idea for a bath was to go down to the cold cellar basement of the old farmhouse; he ran a plumbing line which, fortunately, included hot as well as cold water. There was a little cast iron bowl approximately 24 inches wide on the dirt floor near the water lines.

Each of us boys would step into this cast iron bowl and clean our face with Lava soap. Lava was the only soap we had on the farm. It was intended to clean grease and grime from your hands after working all day in the fields. However, it widely opened up the pores, could actually give you a rash in some portions of the interior part of your thighs, and, in my opinion, was just simply harmful to your health!

Now, the reason I tried to get up early (although it very seldom worked) was because the same water was used for three "baths" in a row; thus, the last "survivor" got to share the Lava bath water with the prior two "*escapees.*"

On those days in the winter when it was 10 above zero, those "sponge" baths generally did not take long; I remember many times high-tailing it back up the old basement steps butt-naked trying to find a heat register to stand over so I could jump-start my heart!

. . . .

MORNING HAS BROKEN

Sometime, during my junior year, I sent ten dollars along with an application to the University of Cincinnati.

This seemed to be my only hope.

Living on the farm, I had never seen, much less visited, the UC campus. I had been to Cincinnati perhaps a dozen times, each time to watch the Reds play baseball at old Crosley Field.

Four weeks after I sent in my application, I got a letter in the mail from the University of Cincinnati.

My hands trembled as I opened the sealed envelope.

The letter read, "Congratulations! You have been accepted into the college of engineering at the University of Cincinnati."

I took the letter behind the old barn and literally sobbed for two hours.

For some high schoolers, being accepted to the college of their choice is probably a very cool moment. For this naive farm kid, it was a miracle!

Now, it was going to be up to me.

Oscar, thank you.

. . . .

ONE FINE DAY

I remember driving home on a beautiful, absolutely stunning, summer evening; I was seventeen; I had just left Martinsville driving over the railroad tracks on Cemetery Road heading back to the farm.

All the windows of the '57 Ford were down; the radio was blaring; the wind was blowing through my hair. Did I mention the radio was blaring!!!

I was in love.

I remember thinking – there will never be another year as cool, as wonderful, as this year.

There will never be another year better than the year I was 17.

. . . .

HE TOUCHED ME

On a beautiful summer night on the banks of a little tributary extending from Lake Cowan, at a Quaker church camp, I surrendered my life to Jesus Christ.

Through the enabling of my friend, Anna Jean Hadley, after reading the first few verses of Genesis with deep devotion, I cried out and asked the Lord to come into my heart.

I immediately felt His presence and fell to my knees.

The seed of Jesus Christ was in me.

I will be more than forever grateful (forever is eternity) to Anna Jean Hadley, who at 18 was beautiful inside and out, and remains so to this day.

I had accepted Jesus Christ as my Lord and Savior.

NOW ALL I DID FOR THE NEXT 7 YEARS WAS PROVE TO HIM THAT HE SHOULD NEVER HAVE ACCEPTED ME AS HIS SON!

■■

DON'T GO BREAKING MY HEART

Martinsville High School

Just great memories.

And then there was the consolidation.

That was a time when little country schools were forced to bundle up and merge with larger school districts.

It was most intimidating for us in the little community of Martinsville to know we were going to be bussed over to the big city of Wilmington for our final year.

My senior year at Wilmington High School went o.k. Most of the kids in Wilmington went out of their way to welcome their country neighbors from the south to the big city.

After almost being SOMEBODY in Martinsville, as a result of being a part of a much larger student body, I returned to being a NOBODY my senior year at Wilmington High School.

Once again, a scum bag.

· ·

WHAT BECOMES OF THE BROKEN-HEARTED?

When I entered the University of Cincinnati, I don't remember being happy much; I do remember a tremendous feeling of loneliness.

I remember four years of having very little self worth.

My self image was of a poor kid who wore the same Big Mac denim shirt daily and a pair of trousers which I had bought from the Salvation Army off Vine Street.

I was not a big man on campus; in fact, I'm probably the only one that knew I was on campus.

· ·

DEAD AIM

When I returned home on Christmas break during my freshman year from U.C., I took my meager belongings upstairs to the bedroom which Bill and I shared.

Once I got to the top of the stairs in the old farmhouse, I opened up the closet door to throw my things in.

I was shocked!

In this oversized closet, somehow, during my three month absence, it had been magically turned into a bathroom!

I ran back downstairs and said, "Mom, that is *really* cool!"

Well, she said, "Honey, we were able to do it and it just seemed to be the right time."

I thought to myself, *O.K., let me get this straight, I leave home and now just seems to be the right time to put in a bathroom*.

Well, I was happy for the remaining family members who had experienced this *lifestyle upgrade*.

It did, however, feel strange.

For the first time in eighteen years, I was actually able to pee inside a house where we lived.

In fact, the first time, I remember being just a bit nervous; I didn't want to mess this up.

I took dead aim.

● ●

STILL NOT GOOD ENOUGH

As you know by now, during my college years, my self-worth was somewhere between the butt of a forty-pound canary and scum on a dirty Cincinnati Vine Street sidewalk.

I think this was one of those incidents that I had suppressed until recently. It just came to me as I was in the process of thinking through what had really occurred during those years off Clifton Avenue.

Late one afternoon, I put in my application and interviewed to become a "Big Brother of America".

After three or four days went by and I had heard nothing, I called the phone number on the brochure.

The person on the other end of the line informed me that, "No, I was not 'big brother' material."

I wasn't even worthy of being a "big brother".

Now, that's cold.

■■

CAN'T TAKE MY EYES OFF OF YOU

It was at the annual December Elks Charity Ball in the old Wilmington High School gymnasium.

I hadn't seen her, but maybe once, since graduation. And now, there she was, with some guy, looking as absolutely beautiful as ever!

Even though I was not with her that night, I could not keep my eyes off of her!

She was absolutely stunning!

■■

BROWN EYED GIRL

That ride back to the farm when I was seventeen with the wind blowing through my hair listening to "Stand By Me" blaring on the radio seemed like a hundred years ago.

Because, then, there she was.

Dollie and I were married nine months after "I couldn't keep my eyes off of her" at that Elks Charity Ball!

I knew she would be a handful as she was escorted up the aisle by her father at the Martinsville Friends Church on that beautiful September afternoon; the wink she gave me from four steps away, assured me that there would never be a dull moment.

I married a beautiful woman, a person with a very strong work ethic who has always demanded the best of her two daughters... and the best of her husband.

She saw something special in me. Finally, the scumbag did something right.

■■

I FALL TO PIECES

I'll never forget the night I graduated from the University of Cincinnati but not because I felt any sense of accomplishment. Unlike many of the kids today, who have family and friends to help them celebrate the victory of their diploma, I had only with me, Dollie, my Dad, Mom, Uncle Chic and Aunt Katie.

After walking across the beautiful turf at Nippert Stadium along with eighteen thousand graduates to receive my diploma, my little family headed back to the tiny apartment on Auburn Avenue where Dollie and I lived my last year of school.

Shortly after receiving the packet with my diploma, I removed the sleeve-I was so excited to see the rewards for working hard the past five years.

I was shocked; instead of a diploma, there was a hand written message that said when I paid the $39 in delinquent bills for parking illegally on the campus, I could pick up my diploma.

We hadn't been back in the apartment ten minutes when my Mother said, "Butch, show me your diploma."

I said, "Mom, it's downstairs in the car; I'll get it in a little bit."

About a half hour later, my Mother said, "Honey, where's your diploma?"

The inside of my tummy began to churn, to hurt, to ache.

My Mother, who was my strongest supporter, who had sacrificed and done without so that her oldest son could be the first Peelle in our family to ever graduate from any institution of higher learning, was going to be so disappointed.

I just felt like the four walls of that little apartment were crushing in on me. Was I going to have to tell her the truth?

Fortunately, she didn't bring it up again that night. Four days later I paid the bill, but I never showed my mother my degree. I was embarrassed and realized...

I was still a scum bag.

●●

THE LONG AND WINDING ROAD

As I neared graduation from U.C., my father had been nearly killed in an automobile accident that February. It was apparent to Dollie and I that we needed to be closer to home, closer to my Mother.

As Bill and Bob observed how their older brother, who had an IQ somewhere between a veg-a-matic and a Phillips screwdriver, could get out of the trenches, they knew that if he could do it, they could do it!

They were both on their way to Ohio State and later to Ohio Northern for law school.

So here I was, during the summer of 1969, looking for employment in the town of Wilmington. As many of you know, we never anticipate coming back home.

But, here again, you don't mess with God.

Looking back, He knew, years before I knew, that for the plan in my life to become a reality, I was going to have to learn how to make seven slang words develop into a real sentence that people could actually understand. Therefore, He opened up the opportunity for me to be a junior high math teacher.

Pretty demeaning, I thought, for a kid that had made every effort to be a teacher's nightmare when I was in school!

●●

I'M PROUD TO BE A COAL MINER'S DAUGHTER

"You don't <u>mess</u> <u>with</u> <u>God</u>."

> *God's plan for your life <u>does</u> <u>not</u> <u>always</u> <u>take</u> <u>you</u> <u>where</u> <u>you</u> <u>want</u> <u>to</u> <u>go</u>.*

How about this for a journey?

She was born and reared, one of six beautiful daughters, in the foot hills of Hazard, Kentucky.

Her daddy pretty much kept the Hazard County boys away with a ball bat or whatever other weapons he had to use to protect his girls!

Elizabeth Looney didn't want to leave Hazard, Kentucky; after all it was her hometown; her family was there and she loved them very much; she had a great life. Even at a young age she was modeling for one of the local clothes shops.

SHE *REALLY* DIDN'T WANT TO LEAVE her comfort zone in Hazard.

BUT SHE DID!!

Because one of her sisters needed her- a sister that lived in Dayton, Ohio- Elizabeth went to Dayton, no questions asked. She didn't have any trouble finding a job at an exclusive men's clothing store.

She met the guy of her dreams, Ernie Looney, who soon became her husband.

For several years, the Looneys had successful businesses and real estate holdings in the Centerville and Oakwood areas. During this time, however, Pastor Looney had been doing a considerable amount of traveling as an evangelist. She was attending revivals all over the United States as she felt called to spread the "Word of God". But, she also missed her babies, Renee, 12, and Joe, 8.

She started praying, *I'll always keep you first GOD and I know we have work to do! Help me so I can do your will and still be close to my family.*

The Lord directed Pastor Looney to the Bloomington Church of God, a small, dilapidated church near the village of Sabina in southwestern Ohio, an old brick building with grass three feet tall and an outside toilet.

SHE *REALLY* DIDN'T WANT TO LEAVE her comfort zone in Dayton.

BUT SHE DID!

Pastor Looney began her ministry here. It lasted until the landlord no longer wanted church services in the building and asked her to go (shortly after, the aging structure was destroyed by a bolt of lightning!).

With no place to go, Pastor Looney was able to obtain permission to preach in an old outdoor theatre on the Sabina fairgrounds where she and her family would shovel the remnants of a certain horse product three times a week so that she could hold worship services in the antiquated fairground bleachers.

From there, she took the gospel to a number of people's homes and then the old VFW building on Dalton Road; later, she had the opportunity to take up residency in a church building on South Walnut Street in Wilmington.

Today, through the power of prayer, walking step by step with Jesus, she holds services in an absolutely stunning church building on the west side of Wilmington.

Her <u>behind the scenes</u> charity work includes combining efforts with local businesses to send trucks loaded with food and supplies to Louisiana in the aftermath of Hurricane Katrina... as well as the local clothing and food pantries which meet the needs of many.

Pastor Looney is an absolutely amazing lady of the highest integrity.

There is no question, that she has been used by the Lord and that her steps have been directed by Him.

GOD'S PLANS FOR YOUR LIFE DO NOT ALWAYS TAKE YOU WHERE YOU WANT TO GO!

And then, again, *you don't mess with God.*

David says: The steps of a good man [woman] are ordered by the LORD; and He delighteth in his [her] way. Psalm 37:23

I CAN HELP

A few days before I was to begin teaching, I happened to run into Gary Kersey at the Plaza Barbershop.

Gary, I understood, was a fine teacher at the junior high school and I was excited to see him! Gary and I had been friends in high school; I always made every effort to eat at the lunch table with him because his story-telling ability had stretched to a high pinnacle by the time he was a senior. By the end of Kerz's last yarn at the lunch table, we would all pick up our trays to leave and in unison say "AHHHH…. Kerz, *come on*!"

As I was about to sit down in the barbershop so Don Holland could work his magic, Gary belted out "Peelle, I was in your classroom today, and you've done <u>nothing</u>!"

I said, "AHHHH… I didn't know school started today!"

He said, "No (as if I was *really* stupid), what I mean is, you've done nothing to decorate your room."

Now, here I am thinking… *I just wanted to teach; I didn't know I needed to be an interior decorator*.

The next day, Kerz and I met in *his* classroom, which looked similar to the Smithsonian Museum of Natural History!

To be sure, Gary Kersey taught me a tremendous amount about speaking in complete sentences and how to generate excitement and enthusiasm in the classroom!

More often than not, over the next five years, Gary and I would meet after school in an empty classroom to exchange ideas on how things went that day; sometimes, after an hour or so, Myron Halley, our junior high principal, would have to remind us: *"it's time to go home, boys"*!

Gary and I would often muse that the kids in our classrooms would "make it *because of* or *in spite of* anything we did!"

I will always be grateful to Gary and the other classroom teachers for their kindness and support at the old Wilmington Junior High School on West Locust Street.

• •

HARD WORK CAN BE FUN

I was shocked!

Being in the classroom with 35 to 40 energetic, enthusiastic 8th graders was a truly remarkable experience. One that I had not counted on!

Each night, I would work until 11pm preparing for each of the five or six classes I would have for the next day.

I wanted every word to be perfect; I wanted every phrase to be perfect; I wanted to have learning take place in that classroom.

We had some good times; many times we'd visit prior to easing into the work at hand, but the kids were enthusiastic, they were wonderful, and it was just five of the most perfect years in my life!

• •

HAPPY TOGETHER

It's interesting how things sometimes can appear to be altered, looking from a different perspective.

One time when I was teaching, the kids were kind of messing with me; one of the boys said, "Mr. Peelle you must really be old!"

I said, "O.K., how old do you think I am?"

He said, "Man, you must be at least 24!"

I said, "Yep, that's exactly what I am, 24."

"How old are you guys?"

Well, almost in unison, "we're 14!"

So, I see, "Let me get this straight. You're 14 and I'm 24.

"Hmmm. . . So, what you're saying is when I'm 75, you're going to be 65. *Who's going to be old then*?"

You should have seen their faces and heard their groans.

"In other words, Mr. Peelle, we're going to be old together; <u>old together with you</u>!????."

●●

I CAN SEE CLEARLY NOW

During the first summer break from the classroom, I worked in a small screw driver factory at the south end of Walnut Street in Wilmington.

I'll never forget my first week.

With a box of handles on my left and a box of blades on my right, it was my job to put the handle and the blade in the proper position so that when the machine clanked together, the blade would slide perfectly into the wooden handle.

About the third or fourth day, I was getting to a point that I thought I was seeing some success. Not near as often did the handle and the blade pop skyward toward the ceiling as they jammed into each other!

I was so proud; so very proud of my accomplishments in just four days.

All of a sudden, breaking my thought process, was Blackie McPherson, the owner of the screwdriver factory.

He said, "You're getting pretty good, aren't you?"

I said, "Yup, I'm really liking this."

He said, "That's good, we're going to shove it up into second gear."

I said, "Wait a minute. How many gears does this thing have?"

He said, "THREE!"

He shoved it into second gear and I almost lost my right hand.

All of a sudden this sucker is clicking quicker … quicker … and quicker … and quicker! Give me a break! And there's still a third gear!

For fifty-four bucks a week, I was risking my limbs, but earning a summer living.

I loved teaching, but after our second child, Carrie, was born, I thought maybe I needed to look for something else.

SECTION II

Today, Expect a Miracle

I'M A BELIEVER

It was during my second excruciating "LIFE-TEST" in the early 80's when I saw a television evangelist deliver a sermon "Expect a Miracle". Our little realty office had only been opened for fourteen months when home interest rates began to accelerate to 16-18% record highs, hostages were held in Iran and our nation was in a stressful, unsure period of time similar to what we remember so vividly going through in 2008, 2009, and 2010!

Shortly after that, on my schedule for each work day, I would write in bold letters: "EXPECT A MIRACLE"!

As the days and weeks went by, in my mind, I had begun to expect a miracle.

In December of 1981, I shared with Dollie that if the real estate market didn't improve by May, 1982, I was going to have to get a *real job*.

In January, 1982, something happened that has never happened before and has never happened for me since: a transaction in which three families bought three homes in a triangular fashion- A bought B, B bought C, and C bought A.

A MIRACLE?!

It was not easy, but that was the beginning of working ourselves out of a 30 month hole.

There has not been a day since where I have not put in bold print on my daily planner: "EXPECT A MIRACLE"!!

•••

THERE'S A KIND OF HUSH

When I was in the second grade, living on our little farm outside of Mowrystown, my friend, Steve Harvey, invited me to stop by on a Saturday. So I drove my little bicycle down Taylorsville Road, across the railroad tracks, turned right and pedaled through the center of Mowrystown, heading south toward Sardinia. The Harvey's had a very pretty place about a mile outside of town.

Steve Harvey was always on the cutting edge. His parents had gotten him a very cool bow and arrow. I had a cool bow and arrow, but it had a *suction cup* which made it difficult to kill wildlife!

Steve and I were playing with his bow and arrow, shooting at a target on a bale of straw when he said he needed to go inside for something. Thus, I found myself alone with this "real" bow and arrow. So I thought, *you know, I wonder what would happen if you shot an arrow straight up in the air*? I assumed the arrow would eventually come back down.

So, with all my might, I shot the arrow straight up into the air. After, what seemed like five minutes, nothing happened. My heart started beating against my chest because something just didn't feel right.

And then, all of a sudden, "SWOOSH!!"

The arrow missed hitting the top of my head by just inches; it was stuck in the ground less than twenty-four inches from my feet.   My heart was really beating now!

For the first time in my life, I thought *something interesting is going on*.

Was I lucky... or *was it a MIRACLE*?!

●●

BACK THE LANE AGAIN

I never will forget the day when the three of us little rug-rats were at home with my Mother and the sky changed from light blue to a very hideous, scary, dark color. Shortly, rain and hail began to thunder down from the sky. To say that my brothers and I were terrified would be an understatement.

My Mother had many idiosyncrasies, which, in retrospect, were not that silly. She made sure that during any storm when there was lightning, thunder and scary stuff, that each of us boys would sit on a pillow, clasping our hands beneath our pillows, while sitting on the couch. I think she explained the reason for this, but for the life of me, I don't remember how this was going to save our lives.

All of a sudden on this particular dark day, we boys, half-scared to death, saw a flame of fire shoot up from right behind the old house. We were even more scared!

My Mother threw on a coat and ran out the back door into this torrential downpour. She grabbed an old metal rod out of the mud.

As my brothers and I looked out the window, fear filled our hearts. My Mother began to approach the flaming electrical wire with this rod. She suddenly put the rod down, grabbed an old tobacco stick (similar to a surveyor's stake but about 36 inches long) and with this stick, separated the two hot wires from each other. The fire stopped.

My Mother, drenched, ran back into the house.

It was much later that evening when the three of us boys, still shaken from what we saw happen during the day, overheard our Mother telling our father, "Hubert, do you realize had I not picked up that wooden tobacco stick but had tried to separate those two live wires with that metal rod, I could've been electrocuted and died in front of the boys?"

That was when I began thinking, *there's something going on in this family. Is it something special? Does it have to do with God?*

GOD KNOWS YOUR HEART

Knowing at a certain point in my life that God was using me to glorify his name, I have asked my Heavenly Father hundreds of times, when I was in prayer with him, "How is it that from early on, you chose me, a reckless sinner, a most unworthy human, a smart-alec kid, a pathetic husband, a not-so-terrific father- how is it that you have chosen me, this most unlikely and unworthy sinner, to promote Your Name?"

My good friend, Pastor Kurtis Summerville, of the Missionary Bible Baptist Church in Wilmington, opened up my eyes one Sunday morning when he said *"God can use you!"*

He went on to say "If God used Moses who committed murder, if God could use Samson the womanizer; if God used David who was an adulterer; if God used Peter who denied Him, then God can use you!!"

"God forgives".

"Man looks on the outside but God looks at your heart"!

Even though I am a highly unworthy, undeserving human, a sinner, a scumbag, *through God's grace*, He has allowed me to be a servant and to bring Glory to His Name.

· ·

How's your heart with the person who just betrayed you, wronged you, or is spreading untrue, unkind gossip about you?

When WORD gets back to you (though the evildoer never suspects his or her "friend" would run straight to you) with the "betrayal" or rumored gossip, the hurt runs deep. Sometimes the anger runs deeper.

Or, how's your heart with the company that just terminated you, broke you financially and left you on the sidewalk to die a miserable death?

When you get a pink slip *or* you are walked to the exit gate escorted by your friend, the hurt, the shame, the anger and the anticipated financial pressures make your head spin into a deep depression.

Now, here's the deal... as difficult and as unnatural as it may be to hear these words, this is what you need to do to get through these things:

1. Forgive... the *person or company* as soon as you possibly can.

2. Pray... for the goodwill, prosperity and future for the person or company as quickly as you possibly can. Do this every day.

3. Do not worry. Do not fret. Be at peace.

> Psalm 37 says:
> *Fret not thyself because of evildoers,*
> *Neither be thou envious against the workers of iniquity.*
> *For they shall soon be cut down like the grass,*
> *And wither as the green herb.*

Whether you still have hurt inside, anger inside or hate inside, be quick to forgive!

Forgiveness doesn't make the person or company right, but it will help set you free. You just don't have the time or the energy to continue being angry: refusing to forgive a person or a company will eat the inside of your gut with bitterness.

In addition to your mental state going awry, soon your physical condition will suffer. Please remember and write down these words:

> Forgiving is the beginning of all healing.

The Bible says: "For if you forgive people of their evil deeds toward you, your heavenly Father will also forgive you."

- -

NUMBER OF <u>HOT</u> REAL ESTATE MARKETING DAYS IN 2008~ <u>29</u>

As a result of the snow, the ice and the sleet, in the early part of 2008, the real estate market in our area didn't even begin to break open until May 1, 2008. On May 29, 2008, the headline from the Wilmington News Journal stated:

"6000 AIR PARK JOBS TO BE LOST"

Thus, we had 29 days of "*hot*" home sales in 2008.

From May 29, 2008 through the remaining seven months of the year, folks in our area were frightened, scared, stressed and in some cases, even worse. Consequently, people were scared to buy homes, cars or almost anything, even if they were in a position to do so.

Thus, anything that did sell after May 29th needs to be classified as a MIRACLE!

- -

I JUST CAN'T HELP BELIEVING

I remember the first time I visited Jim and Gwen Belcher, who owned a country home south of Wilmington on SR 68. They were excited as Jim had recently found a new position in his old hometown in Michigan; with deep faith, they knew their home would sell!

With such deep conviction, I only took a 30 day listing, dated July 28, 2008. Amazingly enough, just 20 days later, Jim and Gwen's country property SOLD!

The new owners, Luroy and Debbie Solsman just *happened to be* searching for that "perfect home and setting" in the country.

MIRACLE?!   I think so.

· ·

SOME KIND OF WONDERFUL

Randy and Connie Vaughn owned a very sharp contemporary style home on the west end of New Vienna, a village south of Wilmington. Randy and Connie were both from well-known families in the Wilmington area; Randy had received an excellent opportunity just days before and it was imperative that Randy get to the west side of Chicago within four weeks.

Their home and property was listed at a fair price. Randy and Connie signed their papers to put their home on the marketplace; their home and property SOLD to a delightful couple, John and Wanda Galliett, just 14 days later!!

Remember, during this time, <u>OTHER</u> <u>HOMES</u> <u>SIMPLY</u> <u>WERE</u> <u>NOT</u> <u>SELLING</u>!! E*xcept, it seemed, only for those folks who needed to relocate for their new jobs.*

MIRACLE?!   I think so.

- -

HE'S GOT THE WHOLE WORLD IN HIS HANDS

Larry and Jackie Stevens are well known to our area. Larry had been with the local Air Park for nineteen years; Jackie is in the public eye as a result of her cheerful assistance and ability to get things done at the Clinton County Recorder's office.

But things were looking very grim for the Stevens'. Larry knew it was just a matter of months before he was going to be terminated.

The day I met with them, the cloud of stress in their family room was so heavy, it would have taken a razor blade to cut through the tension. Prior to the DHL announcement, Larry had already had three stints in his heart; he was so uptight and stressed that I was fearful his heart would explode through the front of his chest.

I was frightened for both of them. Like nearly everyone else in our community, Larry and Jackie were going through a situation they had never been through before.

Just a few months prior to this listing visit, they had shared with me how things were going so well. They were going to be retiring in the next five years and buying that perfect secluded piece of heaven in the hills of southern Kentucky.

And now this.

I left that June day with the listing and in tears. This time it was my turn to have knots in my stomach. I can deal with my own issues. I have peace with my own issues. I have the gift of my heavenly Father on my right side giving me peace within.

But I could not leave Larry and Jackie's house without deep hurt inside the day I listed their home and headed back to the office.

A few weeks later, one of my happiest moments was the day Larry Stevens called and left a message with Nancy, "take our home off the market." In my gut, I felt something positive had happened.

Jackie later told me that Larry had gotten a job in nearby Blanchester, not paying as much as he had been accustomed to, but yet a job.

A couple of months after that, I had the opportunity to enjoy a great visit with Larry in his little building; his little hideaway behind their home. He was so much more relaxed. He was so much more at peace.

I told him, as Joyce Meyer would say, "You're not where you want to be, but you're a lot further along than you used to be."

He agreed. He shared with me about how the last few months had been so tense and stressful that he had to have yet another stint put into his heart. He said, in fact, that the stress and communication breakdown between him and Jackie had caused some hurt for nearly three months during their relationship. Then, he quickly went on to say how much he loved his wife and everything was starting to get better.

His new boss had indicated to him that with his background, there was an excellent chance that he may be named a supervisor in one of the other stores. As we enjoyed our visit, even though there was still much hurt and still some unsettled feelings due to the loss of several thousands of dollars as a result of his termination, he still said "you know, Butch, I still haven't given up on the dream. Jackie and I will have our little piece of paradise someday in the mountains of southern Kentucky."

MIRACLE?!   I think so.

• •

IT'S JUST A MATTER OF TIME

There are many places in the Bible, where it is obvious that our Heavenly Father wants us to have our desires, the desires of our heart; but WE HAVE TO ASK!

In Mark 11:22-24, Jesus says "Have faith in God … *whatever things you desire when you pray, believe that you receive them, and you will have them." (Emphasis mine)*

Also, if you have not read the book "The Prayer of Jabez," by Bruce Wilkinson, you might want to consider it. Simply put, there's this little dude in the book of 1 Chronicles who, with arms stretched to the heavens, prayed these simple four lines:

> *"Oh that thou would bless me indeed;*
> *And enlarge my territory;*
> *That thine hand might be with me,*
> *And that thou would keep me from evil…"*

A little prayer; great stuff.

And finally, Psalm 37: 4-5:

> *Delight yourself in the Lord;*
> *And He shall give you the desires of your heart.*
> *Commit your way unto the Lord; trust in Him;*
> *And He shall bring it to pass.*

And then, sometimes, we ask, we pray and there are times when our prayers don't seemed to be answered, at least in the time frame that *we think they should be*!

Psalm 37:7 is so cool:

> *Rest in the Lord, and <u>wait</u> <u>patiently</u> for Him...*

This is not a call to be inactive, but to *wait patiently* on the Living Lord (for while we are concerned about our future, our Heavenly Father is working behind the scenes to develop the harvest He has already prepared for you).

■■

WAKE UP, LITTLE SUZIE, WAKE UP!

In September of 2004, I received a call from an acquaintance that I had actually known all of my life. On the other end of the telephone, she asked "Do you remember that book you gave me in 1991."

I said, "No Suzie, I don't remember that book."

"Well, "she said, "you said you gave it to about everyone!"

I replied, "Oh, do you mean the book *Creating Wealth* by Robert Allen?"

She said, "Yeah that's it."

I said "Ok."

She said "Well, I'm ready to start now."

I said, "You're ready to start what?"
"Don't you remember in 1991 we looked at two or three homes and kind of talked about things?"

I said, "Ok."

"Well, "she said, I'm ready to start now."

This very attractive high energy optimistic friend bought her first investment property within the next sixty days!

Through the support and help of her banker and friend, John Chambers, she has acquired more investment properties and has probably flipped at least a dozen.

Long story short, *it's never too late*!

Suzie and two of her sons, Jarrod and Joel, have formed a strong business relationship in which they work closely together to improve and increase their holdings. Suzie has a third son, Justin, who is currently serving in the U.S. Marine Corps.

Robert Allen, in his book*, Creating Wealth,* has a graph that shows what can happen when you buy two homes a year for ten consecutive years. According to his book, your net worth will increase considerably during that ten year period.

Because of her relatively late start, Suzie decided to double up on her numbers, and as a result, she has seen the fruits of her labor increase significantly.

For years, Suzie had a burning desire to work the plan she had read in Robert Allen's book.

But, only God knew when it was *time for her harvest*!

As it is written in Psalms 37: *"WAIT UPON THE LORD"*

I'LL BE THERE

About two years after we opened up our office doors, Mary Schneder, secretary, receptionist, bookkeeper (we were such a small office, Mary had to do it all!) came in to my little office and said Butch, "there is an older gentleman out here who says he would like to see you".

I got up, walked out and as I slowly moved toward him he removed from his wallet an old tattered and torn "Butch Peelle business card". I'll never forget that day. He said, "you don't remember me, boy. One day a few years ago, you gave me your business card on the sidewalk in Blanchester and said if I had anything to buy or sell to let you know. My wife and I are getting to a point healthwise where we need to make a change. We would like for you to help us sell our country home and find a home more suitable in town closer to things which we feel we need to be close to.

When he left my office, I felt tears flowing down my cheeks.

A little seed planted years ago had reached its harvest.

You see, God knows our needs, but it's up to each of us to plant the seed.

Nothing can come up, nothing will sprout, and nothing will even grow... unless you plant the seed!

> *Even though God has your harvest available and ready for you, He cannot grant His favor to you until you <u>ask</u> <u>him</u>!!*
> *Until you plant the seed.*

TURN BACK THE HANDS OF TIME

I'm reminded of the fellow that went to Heaven and was met by one of God's angels to begin the journey toward the Heavenly Throne.

As they begin walking, the man says "This is the most beautiful, greenest grass I've ever seen! And the angel replies, "Yes, it's absolutely beautiful isn't it?"

They walked a little further and the man exclaims, "Wow, that is the most beautiful, bluest, peaceful lake I've ever seen!" and again, his heavenly guide nods in agreement.

On down the road, the man sees a big building. It's made of steel. It has no windows, only a small entrance door. "What in the world is that?" he asked. The angel says, "It's just a building. That's all it is. We really need to keep going because your Heavenly Father is expecting you, we need to be on time."

But the man balks. "Wait a minute," he says "can't we just go over to that building and take a quick look inside?"

The angel, losing a bit of patience, says, "Well, come on. If we hurry, perhaps we can take a quick peek."

Inside the building there are rows and rows of boxes. Big boxes. Little boxes. Odd-shaped boxes... "What's the deal with the boxes?" the man asks. The angel explained that there is one box for every person that has ever walked the face of the earth, to which the man then replies, "You mean there is one in here for me?"

"I guess so," says the angel. "They all have names on them."

Like a kid in a candy store, the man ran up and down the aisles. Then he stopped and screamed. "I found my box! I found my box! And it's the biggest box on the shelf!"

He motioned for the angel to come see. "This is wonderful" he said **"I've got the biggest box up here!** Tell me what's in my box! Tell me!!"

The angel replied, "Those are *all the blessings* that your Heavenly Father had for you on earth... but you *never asked Him for them*."

PRAYER CIRCLES

Have you ever gone home after work with something bothering you, something "sticking in your craw". The knots in your tummy are tighter than usual. Something is not quite right.

You think back over the events of the day.

Perhaps it was something that someone said that bothered you. Something you said to someone else that bothered them and later bothered you. Or perhaps it was just an incident or occurrence about a friend or loved one that hurt you deep inside.

Several years ago, I came home from work, exhausted, knots in my stomach, frustrated- just feeling all torn up inside.

About 10:30 that night in the quiet of my little office, my first *"prayer circle"* exploded out of my pen with the words: "What's bothering you?"

I began to list every hurt, disappointment, frustration, and situation that was beating me to pieces and breaking my heart, all at the same time.

When I was through with my list, a certain calm began to slowly come over me. I started at the top and read very slowly over the list which I had just written. Later, I would eventually draw a circle around my "prayer", place a capital G O D on the top of the circle and place the date on the upper right hand corner. Then, I'd place the tablet with the most recent prayer face-up into the right-hand side of my desk drawer and would fall into bed.

I don't know if angels have eyes. I don't know if angels can see. All I know is that what I just did was turn all of my day's hurts, disappointments, ISSUES. . . over to my Heavenly Father.

For the first time in weeks, I slept peacefully throughout the night. For while I was at rest, my Heavenly Father was working through my problems, my hurts and my frustrations.

Now, in the morning, I wake up refreshed with a clean white linen to begin the new day.

Try it...

It's an interesting thing; after a few weeks, you'll find yourself looking back over your Prayer Circles and with near disbelief, you will then see how your Heavenly Father has handled so many of your hurts and situations.

You may even catch yourself whispering aloud, *"So, Lord, that's how you worked that problem out!" "Thank you, Father, for the improvement in Aunt Dottie's health." "Thank you, Father, for working out the loan situation for that young couple." And "Father, what a MIRACLE to work things out so quickly, for Jim and Gwen Belcher, allowing them to relocate to their hometown in Michigan!"*

> *You will find it to be truly amazing as to the kinds of ways your situations have been beautifully resolved.*

WHAT'S LOVE GOT TO DO WITH IT

> Will Rogers said, "The Bible tells us to love our enemies; just for fun, why don't we try it out on our friends for a change!"

Dollie and I had been seeing each other for a short time when I approached her and began to wrap my arms around her.

She said, "What are you doing?"

I said, "ehh, it's called a hug."

She said, "I don't think I do hugs".

I said, "Well let's ease into it and see how it works out."

Today, I have a habit of giving nearly everyone I run into, particularly those that I have a strong loving relationship with, a hug.

As our girls began to get older, we began to do, "group hugs", meaning all four family members would just snuggle in one big wrap-around hug!

Now years later, when we're all together for whatever occasion, before the party breaks up, it has become a tradition in our family that Dollie and I, the girls, their husbands, Dollie's Dad and any nearby grandkids along with guests cozy up for a "**great big group hug!**"

I believe hugs are warm, cuddling and one of the strongest acts of love that one person can show another.

HOLD ME, THRILL ME, KISS ME

The happiest most enthusiastic loveable huggable folks who meet me when I arrive home at 10 o'clock each night are named Skippy and Joey. Skippy and Joey nearly knock me to the floor each night. There is no one that I have met during the day that loves me more unconditionally, wags their tails any harder and licks and slobbers on me any more lovingly than Skippy and Joey.

So, if you don't currently have a devoted pet, consider a little Skippy or a little Joey, or a little kitty who will love and worship you no matter what kind of day you've had or how slowly you drag through the door.

▪▪

LOVE WILL KEEP US TOGETHER

I believe it's a series of little things that reduce stress within you and improves your days, your weeks and the quality of your LIFE.

I believe and have always believed that you and I have a responsibility on a daily basis to give people a "lift along the way", to put "light" in people's faces.

I believe that it's a series of little things, having to do with <u>our focus on giving to others</u> that help alleviate stress and heartache in the day to day trials and tribulations as we walk through this journey called LIFE.

▪▪

I AM A FRIEND OF GOD

There are a lot of people that say they don't read the Bible because they don't understand it; I think it's the part of the Bible they _do understand_ that bothers them!

I'll bet you've already noticed, He didn't call them the *"ten suggestions"*!

There's a little poem that helps us to remember that we *are human* and that we are *not perfect*. Occasionally, we run into someone who really thinks they *are perfect*. Obviously, they believe they have reached a much higher level than the rest of us:

When I say 'I am a Christian' I'm not shouting 'I'm clean living,'
I'm whispering 'I was lost, now I'm found and forgiven.'

When I say 'I am a Christian' I don't speak of this with pride
I'm confessing that I stumble and need Christ to be my guide.

When I say 'I am a Christian' I'm not trying to be strong.
I'm professing that I'm weak and need His strength to carry on.

When I say 'I am a Christian' I'm not bragging of success.
I'm admitting I have failed and need God to clean my mess.

When I say 'I am a Christian I'm not claiming to be perfect,
My flaws are far too visible, but God believes I am worth it.

When I say 'I am a Christian' I still feel the sting of pain...
I have my share of heartaches, so I call upon His name.

When I say 'I am a Christian' I'm not holier than thou,
I'm just a simple sinner who received God's good grace, somehow!
Pastor Looney

TO KNOW HIM IS TO LOVE HIM

Think you're going through a tough time?

Meet my friend, EDWARD CONRAD.

Edward was a good kid.

So were his brothers and sisters.

Edward couldn't understand why his dad and mom didn't seem to want to treat him very well.

He couldn't understand when he was a little kid that one of his parents hit his sister with a baseball bat.

The entire family lived in a little apartment in a city in southwestern Ohio not far from the Indiana line.

Edward could never understand why, at any given moment, his dad would go in to "rages of anger".

So at the age of 14, when Edward got a whipping more severe than any he had ever received before, he ran away from home.

Edward's first night he slept outside with a drunk guy down near the railroad tracks.

Late in the night, he walked the drunk guy to his home where he lived on the other side of the city.

From there, he went to Saint Peters Catholic Church where he slept on the Catholic nun's porch; at daylight, Edward took off walking.

Over the next few weeks Edward slept in a car in one of the local car lots; he was able to find a car which had not been locked and every morning when he would leave, he would leave a back window down just enough so that he could make sure he had a place to snuggle up that night.

Eventually he was found out; the car lot guy called and reported Edward's activities to his dad; his dad immediately took him to the city police station and turned him in. Edward says they locked him up in a little room in the juvenile detention center in the city. He remembers being moved and relocated to Orient State near Grove City.

Over an eight year period, Edward said he first lived in cottage 4, then cottage D, then cottage E and then finally to Dull Hall. After the eight year term at Orient State, Edward was then transported to the Goodwill Dormitory in Columbus; he says some people that worked there were messing with him and he broke out a window to escape.

He was shortly found and was then shipped to the work house jail off Interstate 71, south of Columbus; after a six month stay there he went to a group home in Reynoldsburg, Ohio; from there he spent time at a YMCA in Columbus.

Edward said, "I somehow got a bus ticket and took a Greyhound bus down to Dayton, I did." He and his new friend, Kenny, slept in the parking garage; after that they slept in a car lot in Dayton.

"For awhile we holed up and slept in the Rikes parking garage; shortly after that, I was able to move to the 11th floor of the Dayton YMCA. Somebody got me out and put me in another Group Home out by Good Samaritan Hospital on Salem Avenue."

"After that, somebody put me in a boarding house on Central Avenue. Shortly after that when I was getting off an RTA Bus, a bunch of thugs beat me up very bad; somebody probably thought I had money."

"One of the best things that ever happened to me was when Martha Avey found out and helped me get to the Wilmington Gallup Street homeless shelter. Tony DeBoard was the head of the homeless shelter at that time."

"Then I lived on Vine Street for awhile; after that, my friend, Gary Straight, who worked at the Dayton GM plant allowed me to sleep in his car at night while he was at work. Gary was a guard and when it was time to get off work he would bring me back to Wilmington."

"I made friends with a good guy named Roy Harrison and we lived in a Spring Street apartment together. He's the guy that used to sit on the concrete wall of the Historical Society on Locust Street with his radio. I really miss Roy Harrison."

"I enjoy the Relay for Life for cancer; I hope they find a cure."

"One of my favorite things that I do is with my friend Jim Mason who has got me with the Knights of Columbus; Jim Mason got me started with this nice group of men."

"I believe my very favorite time in my life is now- after I just turned fifty; I guess the happiest time of my life has been the last two years living at Quaker; I know Wilmington is the best place I've ever lived; everyone is so good to me here; I love living at Quaker."

"I know why other people like me so much.

I help other people, I do.

That's what I do.

And like my girlfriend, <u>Mary</u> <u>Johnson</u>, I check for her mail, that's what I do.

 I take out her trash sometimes."

"You treat me like a man, Butch Peelle.

You treat me like a father.

May God bless you, Butch Peelle."

Today upon the bus I saw a girl with golden hair;
She seemed so gay, I envied her, I wished I were so fair.

When suddenly she rose to leave, she hobbled down the aisle,
'Cause she had one foot against a crutch, but on her face a smile.

Oh God forgive me when I whine,
I have two feet, the world is mine.

One day I stopped to buy some things from the boy at the corner store.
He seemed so pleasant as we talked I decided to buy some more.

When the time came that I should leave he seemed unusually kind;
From his grateful words I understood when he said 'ya see, I'm blind'.

Oh God forgive me when I whine
I have two eyes, the world is mine.

While watching children play one day I observed a handsome lad,
Who stood and watched the others run with a look that appeared quite sad.

I didn't know quite what to do so I motioned to the dear,
Then I slowly perceived his plight and realized he could not hear.

Oh God forgive me when I whine,
I have two ears, the world is mine.

With feet to take me where I go,
With eyes to see a sunset glow,

With ears to hear what I ought to know,
Oh God forgive me when I whine.

I'm blessed indeed,
The world is mine!

Author Unknown

Think your having a bad day?!
Look up into the Heavens.
*Thank God for your **many blessings.***
Look around,
It won't take long to find someone who has gone
through a worse time than you have.

SECTION III

A Salesperson's Walk of Faith

Never Give Up

HELP!

Dollie and I had been married for a couple of years; I was in my second year teaching in the junior high school.

It appeared to me, that those people who owned their own home, had a sense of belonging, had a sense of community, had a family pride as they were rearing their children. Probably most importantly, they were paying THEMSELVES every month and not their LANDLORDS!

Dollie and I fumbled around with this for several months. We called two or three realtors who didn't seem to take much of an interest in our situation. We had heard about a guy who made home loans and so we thought, well, maybe this is the place to start so we set up a meeting with him.

At 5:00 P.M. on a Friday afternoon after school, Dollie and I met him at the little Savings and Loan; after about six minutes, he stood straight up, and as he was walking out of his office, leaving the two of us sitting, he said, "If you people ever have any money, come back and see me."

As we are leaving, I, being the head of the household, felt like a piece of scum.

I think, perhaps, the best thing I do, as a real estate broker, is get hundreds of couples and single folks into their first homes.

Even if there's an issue on their credit, even if there's an issue on their "time on the job"-no matter what might be slowing them down today, we're going to develop a plan. We're going to develop a plan that within the next three, six, nine or twelve months, we can get them in a new home!

We never will allow any couple to leave our office without, giving them at least, "a plan of action."

At the very least, we always leave them with a ray of hope.

Some eight months later, Dollie came home and said that Carl and Rowena were going to sell their home; I said, " duhhh. . .do you think they'd sell it to us?"

The long and the short of it was Carl and Rowena were in their 60's, retiring, and were moving to a mobile home park south of town.

With the help of our parents loaning us $800 (I thought they gave it to us but Dollie paid them back five years later), we were able to buy this cute, two bedroom home on the north side of town.

We sold the home six years later for $11,000 more than we paid for it.

At the time, making $6,500 teaching school, there were days when I was barely able to put food on the table, much less have a savings of $11,000.

With the $11,000, we put that as a down payment on a larger one floor plan home with a living room *and* a family room.

For the first two years we lived there, we didn't have the means to purchase any furniture for the living room, but we had the home!

Because we did reach higher, it was a home that served Dollie, Tracey, Carrie and I well for nearly twenty years.

Sometimes it pays to "Reach for the Stars!"

Even if it means not having any furniture in your living room!

••

FAKE IT 'TIL YOU MAKE IT!

On June 1, 1974, I went into the real estate business, joining the Bailey-Murphy Real Estate Company on Sugartree Street in Wilmington.

I had never listed a home in my life.

I had never sold a home in my life.

Emmett Bailey was the Broker. His son David Bailey was in the front office. T. Donaldson, was in the third office. Joe Phillips was in the fourth office and they cleaned out a small room that had primarily been used for storage and put me in what was now known as the fifth office.

Thus, I was the fifth fiddler in the <u>fifth</u> and <u>smallest</u> <u>Realty</u> <u>office</u> <u>in</u> <u>town</u>! I had been in the real estate business all of five days when Emmett Bailey asked me to help him pound in a sign across town on East Vine Street. Frank Shaw, a neighbor, came over and visited with us as we pounded the sign into the ground. He had seen my announcement and photograph in the newspaper and asked me how I liked my new job.

"It's great!" I answered.

"How can it be great?" Frank shot back, "You've only been doing it for five days!"

> *"We judge ourselves by what we are capable of doing,*
>
> *while other's judge us by what we have already done."*

I WILL SURVIVE

Those early years in real estate were rough!!

In those early months, there were only two people who knew I was in the real estate business and that was me and my wife and there were some days she <u>wasn't</u> <u>too</u> <u>sure</u>! The first year was a tremendous struggle- a tremendous test of faith- there were many days in those early months when I would shut the door of my little office in the old Bailey Murphy Company building- swivel my chair around and just stare at one particular corner of the office where I would pray, asking God if this was the plan he had for my life- if this was *really* what He wanted me to do.

In those days, there were no Tommy Hopkins training sales tapes.

There were no Zig Ziglar motivational tapes.

In searching libraries and book stores in 1974 I could find very little information on the topic of sales techniques.

So I did what all good sales people were told to do- go out and *see the people, see the people! See the people*!!

At the time, it didn't seem like a very scientific approach.

I knocked on doors- I had a lot of extra time to "<u>see</u> <u>the</u> <u>people</u>!"

I would drive out to the country side and visit with my farm friends; really good guys that would put up with me. I'd stop by and visit with Ivan Myers, Pete Hertlein, Wayne Hagemyer, Alan Bradshaw, David Miars, Forest Skidmore, Jim and Joann Parker, Karl and Marie Stroud, Rick Moyer and many others who would put up with me whenever I would pop in.

My goal for those first two years was to be thought of in the same aura as the two leading real estate residential brokers in the Wilmington area market place. I wanted to be thought of in the same breath as Arthur Borton and Stanley Kellough!

They were the top dogs! They worked 50 to 60 hours per week! Both had a high level of integrity and trust in the Wilmington community and together sold 80% of the homes in town.

In my mind, I visualized myself being that third option. Within twenty-four months, that's where I wanted to be!

Even though I didn't know it, by <u>seeing the people</u>, I was <u>sowing some seeds</u>!!

. . . .

IT'S ONLY MAKE BELIEVE

I began to visualize myself being successful, being an Arthur Borton, being a Stanley Kellough.

In the book of Proverbs, it states "As a man thinketh in his heart, so is he."

In addition to visualizing the person I wanted to be, I knew I needed to play the part in other areas. Dollie and I traded in the prettiest candy apple red Chevrolet Camaro coupe (the nicest car we'd ever owned) for an older blue 4-door sedan. I understood that to be in the real estate profession, one <u>must</u> have a 4-door automobile.

. . . .

I'VE BEEN LONELY TOO LONG

Week one went by. Week two, nothing happened. Neither did week three or four or five. Nearly every afternoon for at least a few minutes, I would pull my little office door shut and just stare at the corner of the wall, depressed, rejected and wondered what I was even doing in there; I'd just think and pray, think and pray.

The sixth week, someone had told me there was a little old lady by the name of Jesse Coddington and she had a modest house on Grove Street that she was thinking about selling.

So planning for the next day, I wrote on my list of things to do, that consisted of one thing... call Jesse Coddington. So the next day I went down through my entire list of things to do that consisted of one thing... call Jesse Coddington.

So about 9:15 in the morning when I got to the office, I thought about calling Jesse but I didn't think the time was psychologically *just right*. At 10am, it just didn't seem quite right, but by about 11am, I finally worked up the courage to do that one thing on my list... call Jesse Coddington.

I called. My hand was literally shaking on the phone. I said Mrs. Coddington, "my name is Butch Peelle and I sell homes. I heard that you might be considering . . . . and she stopped me in midsentence without giving me an opportunity to finish as she said in a jittery voice "Stanley Kellough is *my* Realtor." **CLICK!** Don't you think that didn't carry over for the next week as far as my state of depression and rejection were concerned!

About two weeks later, Eleanor, the receptionist for our office buzzed me and said there is a lady on line two who wants to speak to you; I was excited, a real phone call (you see, that first year, I couldn't wait for all of the sales people to leave the office which they generally did around 5:30; because, I would then stay until 9:30 or so trying to pick up any lead I possibly could).

I picked up the phone and this familiar voice said, "Are you Butch Peelle?" I said, "Yes."

She said, "You don't know me; my name is Jesse Coddington and somebody gave me your name; I have a house to sell at 305 Grove Street and I wondered if you would be interested in stopping over to see me?"

For those of us who have been in the real estate business for some time, we know these kinds of silly, crazy (miracles?) are so commonplace that it is almost funny- one day, absolute rejection; the next day, absolute adulation.

I did visit with Jesse, handled the sale of her home and got her involved in another home on Belmont Avenue.

Two years later, on her nursing home bed, as she was gasping for air, she signed the deed related to the sale transfer of her Belmont home.

As I walked away from the old infirmary on Fife Avenue where she laid in an old metal hospital bed, I remember thinking that "today, Butch Peelle is Jesse Coddington's realtor; it was I in whom she had put her TRUST."

I got into my automobile with the warm feeling of pride that Jesse and I were more than just friends.

Two days later, Jesse passed from this world to the next.

∎∎

PUT ME IN COACH, I'M READY TO PLAY

Fifteen months after playing the fifth fiddler on the fifth chair at the Bailey Murphy office, I transferred to the largest company in town, Darbyshire and Associates, Inc. where I became the twenty-fifth fiddler in the largest office in town!

Shortly after, I heard about a fellow who had a two day seminar titled, "How to list 50 homes in 50 weeks." That seemed unbelievable to me so I drove the two consecutive days to a Holiday Inn near the Dayton airport. One of the things he said was if you didn't pass out at least 1,000 business cards every three months, you weren't being effective with your cards!

I started leaving them at restaurants, putting them in the "Real Estate" section of phone books in phone booths, giving one to nearly everyone I ran into, and, saying something like, "Hi, my name is Butch Peelle. I sell real estate. If you know of anyone interested in buying or selling or if you go to church with anyone interested in buying or selling a home, I sure would appreciate it if you would think of me!"

And I would be on my way to the next unsuspecting person who was going to be given a "Butch Peelle" business card!!

....

I DID WHAT THE FAILURES ARE AFRAID TO DO!

A few months later, in a 1977 copy of a little magazine called, *Success Unlimited,* I read about this good looking beach boy attired realtor; the title of the article was *I Did What the Failures Are Afraid to Do!* It was written by a young man by the name of Rick Byers. Rick Byers indicated that he was voted the most likely to fail- out of a graduating class of 154, he said he ranked 153 scholastically.

He said after he graduated, he spent three years in Vietnam as a paratrooper, returned to Pennsylvania and eventually hitchhiked out to California where he was accepted at Golden West College in Huntington Beach. While working out at the gym one afternoon, he met a Realtor from Century 21 who encouraged him to go to real estate school.

When he began real estate, in his first year, he knocked on an average of 800 doors a month. Rick Byers said that "those who don't make it in real estate don't work at it!" He said "you've got to love to work! You must be willing to sacrifice- to work 20 hours a day if you have to! You don't just work an 8 to 5 day and lay around the house all weekend. Those who make it are working late into the night. You must *do what the failures are afraid to do*!"

He went on to say, I have a telephone in the bathroom of our office, I dress in wild Beach boy attire (everyone else out here dresses up in suits, that's why we dress different!).

Also, he went on to say that he gave each of his sales people a small bronze plaque which is engraved, "BUSINESS IS SLOW FOR SLOW PEOPLE"!

I took the things I learned in that seminar and from Rick Byers seriously and **began to apply them**.

At the end of that first full year with the Darbyshire Real Estate Company in 1977, I was the No. 1 producer in the town's number one office!!

WE'VE ONLY JUST BEGUN

On September 11, 1978, Ken Lundy and I opened up an office in an old termite infested house on Rombach Avenue. We called ourselves Peelle Inc. Realtors.

Shortly thereafter we expanded to become Peelle & Lundy, Inc. and have been in the same location (though now in a more modern real estate building) for more than thirty years.

Early on, Homer Lundy (my uncle who had sold his 'men's clothing store') joined us; *with the exception of a couple short periods, the three of us made up our "sales force" for several years. About the time Homer was considering retiring, Matt Williams joined us; Ken, Matt and I were the mainstay for sometime after that; we've always had full time salespeople.*

At the time we opened the doors, since most of the real estate folks in our area wore casual attire, Ken, Homer and I decided we would emulate the idea of Rick Byers and do something different.

We began wearing dark blue suits, driving blue automobiles and utilizing *triangular* blue and gold "for sale" signs.

We also installed a telephone in our bathroom!

During the first few weeks, we would conduct business with our $200 "cardboard" desks which we had acquired at an outlet in Cincinnati. We would be open through the week. Friday evening we would shut down for the week-end, protect the cardboard desks with plastic covering and begin scrubbing, painting and cleaning the old house we'd bought. Late Sunday night, we would uncover the cardboard desks and get ready for whatever business might come our way on Monday morning.

At the time, this old two story house was the only property we could find that was zoned for 'business'. I'll never forget how grateful we were the night that Virgil and Charlotte Reinsmith came by. They had been to a wedding. They looked like two movie stars out of People Magazine. Charlotte was stunning and Virgil was a handsome dude in his wedding tuxedo!

In less than two hours, Virgil had ripped out the entire old kitchen where the reception area was to be (tuxedo and all!).

Without their extra enthusiasm and support, I'm not sure we would have ever got off the bubble in that old building.

YES, I'M READY

Several years ago, Mary Schneder, who had been directing our office for over ten years, made the decision to leave our office and the day-to-day stress and pressure that was part of the job.

Mary had absolutely terrific natural people skills and her absence would leave a large void in our little office.

Thus, the search was on. For over a month, Ken, Matt and I visited with and interviewed over thirty possible replacements.

All could type, most could transcribe, and a few could take shorthand. Several applicants rose to the top, but we remained hesitant.

In a small office like ours, each person is critical. The person we hired would be the person that would answer the phone, the person who would welcome folks to our office, the person who would type a majority of the paperwork and handle the multiple listing service and advertising.

You can teach someone to type. You can teach someone to take dictation. You can teach someone to take shorthand. But, YOU CAN'T TEACH A PERSON TO SMILE, TO CARE, TO BE SENSITIVE TO THE NEEDS OF OTHERS...

In Jonda Towner, I saw those things that you *can't teach*.

Even the day following the interview, both Ken and I received a very well-typed letter from Jonda thanking us for seeing her and reaffirming her desire for the position.

Jonda now jokes about her short interview. "You asked if I could type, but you never asked me how fast!"

Apparently, I didn't ask her how fast she could transcribe and take shorthand either!

Jonda first made an impression on me when I ordered a Big Mac and fries at the

local McDonalds. She was working behind the counter when my order took a little longer than she thought it should have. She slung the fries that had been sitting on my tray into the trash! Then, as my Big Mac came up, she gave me a new hot, fresh, order of fries. She said, "I wasn't going to let you eat those cold ones!"

A few years later, she was working at the Fifth Third Bank in Hillsboro. When I stopped at the drive thru, she greeted me with a great big smile.

Both times, Jonda made me feel like I was "SOMEBODY!"

Jonda's beginnings were somewhat modest; both of her parents passed at much too young of an age. She used to ask "why do things like that happen to me?" OR "why did something work out for another person that didn't work out for me?" But, no more.

She has been the captain guiding our small ship for the past 18 years. She knows each of our strengths and she actually counsels *us*, helping us work through sales issues or situations we face. She is most loyal.

The way Jonda presented herself during her original interview was a prime example of "Fake It 'til you Make It!"

Years later, Jonda told us that her sister, Jana, had actually typed the "thank you" letter!

Talk about "FAKIN' IT!!"

YOU'LL NEVER WALK ALONE

Five years ago I was approached by a well-known realtor in our area who asked if he could spend a day with me, just being with me, watching what I do and how I do it. He said he would pay $500 for this time we had together. I explained to him that I would be happy for him to join me for a day but I did not want to take his money.

During the time I have been in business, I have been given so many opportunities; I have been given so much from others, I have had many people who have come up to me over the years to tell me they pray for me. For their prayers, I am humbled and thankful.

When we are given so much, it is our duty to give back a hundred fold. There will be information in this section which I pray will help assist and improve the attitude, production and the heart of the salesperson who reviews and studies this information. For the price of this book, you'll get more training tips, sales tips and language techniques than my friend would have learned with me in that one day.

But first, let me tell you what *I didn't know*.

YOU SHOWED ME

It was a year after Ken and I had opened up our office doors in the little house on Rombach Avenue that I first learned how much *I didn't know*.

Prior to entering the real estate business, with much regret, we had traded our beautiful candy apple red Chevrolet Camaro for a used 4-door blue sedan; a year later I traded the blue car in for a newer cream-color 4-door; it was beautiful automobile. A year later, I traded that car in for a one-year-old silver 4-door Chevrolet Impala automobile- a real stunner.

In the summer of 1978, Dollie and I, by happenstance, stopped by the Jim Cook GMAC dealership on the west side of town (where the Phillips Insurance office is located today).

The company (now Bush Auto Place) was known for its likable, lovable sales folks who were there to have a good time, not pressure you, but assist you in making the right decision.

That night one of those eager, fun loving sales folks suggested that Dollie and I take a drive in this beautiful black four door luxury Buick automobile which we did. Wow, what a smooth ride. Mr. Cook's wife, Carol, had been driving this car for the past few weeks.

It was still a brand new car! We took it back and thanked them for their courtesies.

Dollie and I both knew we would never own anything as nice as a four door Buick luxury automobile.

The next morning about 11, Randy Moore (who was ten years younger than me and had just started in sales) happened to pop by our office. Randy came in, sat down and said "what did you think of the Buick last night?"

I said "Man, what a satin finish ride- smooth as silk, Randy!"

He then went on to ask what I thought of that two-inch plush leather top. I said I'd never seen anything like it; that was the most beautiful finish to the top of an automobile I have ever seen! He said what did you think of those twelve speakers in that car. He said " Sound comes from everywhere. It sounds like you're right in the middle of a Mick Jagger concert!" I said, "Randy, you are absolutely correct; it was the most gorgeous sound system I have ever heard in an automobile." He then asked, "What about those plush seats?" I said "Plush, those suckers just kind of wrap around you and make you feel like you're part of the car; unbelievable!"

"Well" he said, "let me ask you just one quick question; *with the exception of the price, is there any other reason you'd hesitate to go ahead and buy that car today?*"

I was astounded; I was mortified; with the absolute softest, most beautiful language techniques I had ever heard, Randy Moore had me where he wanted me. And he knew it!

I wanted to hurt him.

Finally, sheepishly, I said "Randy, nope that is the only reason I would hesitate to buy that beautiful car."

"Well" he said, "if we do the arithmetic and we can work out the monthly investment so that it's something you can live with, would you go ahead with it?" I said "Randy, if you can work out the arithmetic on that car so that I can afford it, I would love to have an automobile of that stature!"

That very evening, I drove that stunning black four door Buick luxury automobile off the lot.

Randy Moore had taught me more that day about language techniques than I had learned in my previous years of selling.

• •

AIN'T NO MOUTAIN HIGH ENOUGH

If you're going to be a great one; if you're going to be a professional in the world of sales, you have much work to do! I look at folks getting into the real estate business and I marvel at how they think it's going to be such an easy ride. They think they're going to get wealthy overnight and within the next thirty six months, be retiring on a small island in the Bahamas.

If doctors and surgeons earn $500,000 and up and it takes them years and years of intensive classroom study, then you're not going to be a money-producing machine in the real estate business unless you learn that you need to study and work hard!

For any one starting out in the world of sales, the first book that I would buy and memorize is George Gardner's classic written years ago titled *How I Sold a Million Dollars of Real Estate in One Year* (that would be the equivalent of selling ten million dollars of real estate today!).

After that, I recommend a little book written by Peter B. Kyne, published by William Randolph Hearst in 1921 called *The Go-Getter*. Then, there's Jerry Bresser's early book on language techniques; I would memorize the first two chapters.

Then, read any of Zig Ziglar's books regarding selling, motivation, attitude- anything you can get your hands on by Zig! Also, there's Tommy Hopkins' book that has sold well over a million copies, *How to Master the Art of Selling*. If you're in the world of sales, or *just in the world*, I believe the very best book ever written that will lift you to the next level of any job is Dale Carnegie's classic, *How to Win Friends and Influence People*. Even though it was written in 1935, it is still a timeless wonder regarding people skills.

THE FOUNDATION BUILDING FIRST YEAR

If you're just now entering the world of sales, here's a sheet for you to work through.

1. TO BE A GOOD SALESPERSON, YOU FIRST MUST BE A _____ _____.

2. PEOPLE DO NOT CARE HOW MUCH YOU _____, UNTIL THEY KNOW HOW MUCH _____ _____.

3. SELLING IS _____% UNDERSTANDING HUMAN BEINGS AND _____% PRODUCT KNOWLEDGE.

4. THE KEY TO SUCCESS IN SELLING IS: _____ the _____.

5. THE GREATEST DESTROYER OF SALES: _____ _____.

6. FEARS ARE CREATED BY THE PICTURES PAINTED BY THE WORDS THAT WE USE, USE SOFT WORDS:

Commission   _____

Cost or Price   _____

Down Payment   _____

Monthly Payment   _____

Contract   _____

Buy   _____

Sold   _____

Deal   _____

Sign here   _____

Problem   _____

7. MAKE IT EASY FOR _____ TO _____.

8. MAKE IT EASY FOR _____ TO _____ _____
_____ _____.

9. ALWAYS TRY TO ASK AN ALTERNATE OF CHOICE QUESTION (TRY NOT TO ASK A QUESTION WHERE THE ANSWER CAN BE "NO"). For example: WHAT TIME OF THE DAY IS GENERALLY BETTER FOR THE TWO OF YOU: MORNING, AFTERNOON, OR EVENING.

SINCE EVENING IS BEST FOR YOU, WOULD WEDNESDAY OR THURSDAY OF THIS WEEK BE BETTER?

THURSDAY, THAT'S GREAT, WHAT WOULD BE BEST? WHEN DO YOU BOTH GET HOME? DO YOU WANT TO DO IT BEFORE OR AFTER YOUR SUPPER? WOULD 6:00 BE ACCEPTABLE OR WOULD 7:00 BE BETTER FOR YOU?

10. THE MOST SOOTHING AND COMFORTING FOUR WORDS YOUR CUSTOMER CAN EVER HOPE TO HEAR: _____ _____
_____ _____ !

··

SOMETIMES WE GET CAUGHT UP IN DOING THINGS THE WAY THEY'VE ALWAYS BEEN DONE!!

There was a newlywed couple celebrating Thanksgiving. As she was about to put the ham in the oven, she cut the end of the ham off. Her husband inquired as to why she cut the end of the ham off. She replied, "I cut the end of the ham off because my mommy cut the end of the ham off."

He said let's call your mommy and see why she always cut the end of the ham off. So she called her mommy and her mommy said I cut the end of the ham off because *my mommy* cut the end of the ham off.

Well the bridegroom said to his wife, let's call grandma and see why she cut the end of the ham off. So they dialed her long-distance and got grandma on the phone. They said, "Grandma, on Thanksgiving Day, why did you cut the end of the ham off?" Grandma replied, "I cut the end of the ham off because *my roaster was too small*."

Ray Sarkees, a real estate practitioner with the Bennett Realty Company, taught me a valuable lesson about not having to do things the way I always thought they should be done!

Ray called and said I have a verbal offer on your house on St. Rt. 730. I said, "Ray, we've always made it a practice not to work with verbal offers; if they are serious, they can make an offer in writing on a purchase agreement so I can meet with my folks face to face and try to work this thing through in a business-like manner." Ray said, "Well I think maybe we might eventually be able to pull this together." He said "let's just keep the lines of communication open!"

Ray Sarkees hit me over the head with a two-by-four that day!

I did exactly what he suggested. What could it hurt? I called my folks on the phone and said I don't think we'll get too far with this, but some folks have made a "verbal" offer on your property.

They said, "Well, you know we're not going to be able to take that." I said, "I agree, but let's at least KEEP THE LINES OF COMMUNICATION OPEN." Eventually, Ray Sarkees folks came up a little; my folks came down a little and even though I don't make a practice of doing this, Ray taught me from that day forth, no matter what kind of an offer comes floating in, at least KEEP THE LINES OF COMMUNICATION OPEN!

Here I was still cutting the end of the ham off, just like grandma, because that's the way I'd always done it!

Old goats can learn a lot from new pups.

••

EVERY NIGHT, JUST BEFORE YOU'RE ABOUT TO LEAVE THE OFFICE…

MAKE ONE MORE CALL!!

Shortly after I entered the real estate profession, I heard a speaker who was a successful realtor from an adjacent county, say that one of the things that she thought was very important was, just before she left her office at night, no matter how exhausted, no matter how late, she would make ONE MORE CALL!

Now, I thought to myself-WOW! That's an additional 300 phone calls a year!

Now, as always, I'm always taking a good idea a step further!

I began making two extra phone calls a night!

Tonight, as I have just completed my tomorrow's schedule and am ready to turn off the lights, I *now* make 3 additional calls!

No matter how late!!

That is over 1,000 additional calls a year!

I believe it truly is the <u>little</u> <u>things</u> that make the <u>big</u> <u>difference</u> in your profession, in your LIFE.

• •

I'D RATHER BE LUCKY THAN GOOD

This simple question has allowed me to put more transactions together than any other single question I have ever asked.

The question which has been the most important question I have ever asked actually happened by accident. It happened years ago when a young pilot with Midwest Airlines named Steve McBee came in the office on a Sunday afternoon with his father. Steve was a great kid, probably twenty-two years or so and his father was equally a gentleman; I was doing paperwork on a Sunday afternoon in the old Rombach Avenue termite infested building with the door open to get some light and a bit of a breeze. Up the back stairs leading to the rear door, I heard footsteps.

I showed them into my little office, asked them to make themselves at home.

After a couple minutes of chatting, I learned that dad and son had been searching all week-end for the perfect little home. As they were leaving town, they saw our sign and decided to stop by; it was obvious they were tired, irritable, exhausted, and had not been having much fun. I decided to change that.

98

Almost by accident, I blurted out *"Have you seen a home this weekend that was very close to what you're looking for, but for some reason you didn't go ahead and try for it?"*

Well, for the next 10 minutes, they both raved and talked, almost at the same time, about this one particular home over on N. Spring Street which they thought was for sure the perfect home; however, after offer, counter offer, counter-counter offer, they were unable to come to an acceptable price; they thought the price of the home was still too much!

Most times, as I knew the home, I would have found a way to get the transaction resolved. However, in this case, as it so happened, I had just listed another home which I thought was actually a better, stronger home, a cuter home, for the price.

I said to them, "I have only one home which I believe is very close to what you are looking for; I just put it on the market yesterday afternoon; it will only take us fifteen minutes to see it and then you can be on your way back to Cleveland."

They readily agreed; after what they'd been through that weekend, another fifteen minutes was not going to hurt anything!

I made a quick phone call to the owners, scattered them out to grab a bite to eat, and then opened the front door for Steve and his father.

Forty-five minutes later, after putting the finishing touches on the paperwork, Steve and his father, exhausted, but with broad smiles, were leaving Wilmington knowing they had their arms wrapped around a home that both of them felt very good about.

There are a hundred other great questions.   I think this may be my favorite, probably because it happened by accident.

GETTING TO KNOW YOU, GETTING TO KNOW ALL ABOUT YOU

Sometimes I think it's a shame that real estate folks think that their job is to put on a tap dance and ramble on and on about their particular interests, their hobbies, their families, their dog's names, and every great thing they ever did. Actually, the opposite is true.

The very best sales persons see themselves as doctors or visualize themselves as attorneys, seeing themselves as professional problem-solvers. They ask questions. They shut up. They listen.

> *The biggest single area most of us, as sales practitioners need to work on is to "SHUT UP and LISTEN!"*

Then they write down the response. They continue to ask questions until they have isolated four or five of the very best perfect homes which are available that these folks might be interested in.

Always show the prospective buyer one home that is exactly like the home they described to you that they would <u>not</u> buy.

Also, consider showing your prospective buyer at least one home that is pricier than what they had indicated to you, but does include ALL THE GOOD THINGS that they are seeking; thus, if they really want the home that they hope to find, you may find that the money ceiling was their ideal hope, but that they would be willing to pay more for the perfect home with which they fall in love.

> *Your short cut is to match people to homes, <u>not</u> homes to people.*

If you are going to be a professional, you must visualize yourself as a professional. George Gardner, in his classic book, says "I maintain that the top producer is the top producer because he pays attention to the LITTLE THINGS." He then lists the following as the duties of a practitioner:

1. He (or she) leaves for the office each morning well groomed and well dressed.

2. He has left his personal problems and personal gripes locked in a closet somewhere.

3. He puts a smile on his face, and speaks gently and politely.

4. Throughout the day the key word is courtesy. He opens doors, says "thank you" and "if you please," and "it's been my pleasure."

5. He keeps his car clean and his conversation the same.

6. He is a good listener and a willing advisor.

7. He gives a helping hand, praises his company, and boosts his community.

8. He walks briskly and drives alertly.

9. He attends church, serves on civic projects, and supports charity groups generously.

10. He deals only in facts and treats all men and women equally.

11. His appearance, his words, and his actions are always a credit to his profession.

12. He stands proud, he looks successful, he stands out in his community.

13. He is made up of equal parts of knowledge, training, dedication, and compassion, *all glued together by a multitude of little things*.

Mr Gardner concludes this section by saying, "I guarantee that it will be greatly to your advantage if you 'think little'. It just may be what a real estate person is all about."

GAMES PEOPLE PLAY

Even a fish wouldn't get in trouble if he kept his mouth shut!!

Benjamin Franklin said, "I will speak ill of no man and all the good I can of everyone."

Confidentiality is a key component of keeping your integrity as a professional. You are in a position that you may know personal information. For goodness sakes, KEEP YOUR MOUTH SHUT!

Some folks, perhaps because of their insecurities, perhaps because they just don't know any better, or perhaps because they want to look big in front of someone else, just simply struggle with KEEPING THEIR MOUTH SHUT.

Credibility will suffer immensely if you have "hoof in mouth" disease.

"THE HARDER YOU WORK, THE LUCKIER YOU'LL GET!"

These two brothers went to Antioch School in their first and second grades; they were tossed over to the New Vienna Elementary School which they attended through 7th grade; after that they went to Wilmington for a while, but as they both said in unison, "we didn't like school very much".

What they didn't mind doing, was hard work.

Shortly after dropping out of school, Jeff and James both worked at Frisch's where they did a variety of chores; they would mop and clean the floors at night, being the only two left in the restaurant.

For five years, they delivered pizzas for Dominos.

Their father then helped them get a job at the Blanchester Foundry; the memories were really coming back when they said "when we had to pick up those molds, they were RED HOT!"

With the money which they had saved working at Frisch's, delivering pizzas for Domino's and for the short time at Blanchester Foundry, they were able to buy their first investment property at age 34.

I said "that was pretty good; you guys made the most money by delivering pizzas?" They looked at each other and said "probably". I said "about how much do you think you saved delivering pizzas for those five years?" They kinda looked at each other and said "we saved enough that we could pay cash for four homes to get our business started."

Over the past years, Jeff and James Frost have made a science of purchasing homes in need of considerable repair and through hard work (as well as trial and error) have developed the knack of beautifying these properties into "model" homes.

Working like dogs, these brothers have taken the art of investing and reselling to another level.

Jeff and James have had a remarkable run!

> **And finally, in sales as well as in life,**
> **there are no short cuts for SUCCESS!**

DON'T YOU QUIT!

When things go wrong as they sometimes will,
And the road you're traveling seems all uphill
When the funds are low and the debts are high,
When you want to smile, but you have to sigh
When care is pressing you down a bit,
Rest if you must, but don't you quit

Success is failure turned inside out
The silver tint of the clouds of doubt
And you never can tell how close you are
It may be near when it seems afar
So don't you quit, though the pace seems slow
For you may succeed with another blow!

Author Unknown

DON'T EVER GIVE UP!

Even before our first grandchild, Peyton, was able to walk, much less form words, I would look him in the eyes and say, "Peyton, don't ever give up!"

Paige and Parker have heard the same message. I didn't really know how much an impact this utterance had until recently when Dollie and I were at a Peelle family gathering and my little nephew, Eli Peelle, three years old, looked at me dead-on and said "<u>DON'T</u> <u>EVER</u> <u>GIVE</u> <u>UP</u>!"

Someday, it will be my prayer that when Peyton, Paige, Parker and Eli are trying out for first-string football quarterback, baseball pitcher for the Varsity team, a leading role in a high school musical or running for Senior class president, I hope in the back of their minds that they will hear me whispering *"Don't ever give up!"*

SECTION IV

You Gotta Have Goals!

DREAM GREAT DREAMS!

Years before I became the number one real estate salesperson in Clinton County, I had visualized myself <u>already</u> <u>there</u>!

Fourteen months before this book was published, I visualized the book completed. To help emphasize, I drew a *crude* cover for the book. Granted, it's not a work of art. But it is me reaffirming to myself at the top of my lungs: "This, I'm going to do"! With the DHL fiasco, presidential elections and national economy in the toilet, *people need a lift!* people need ways to handle hurt, disappointment and grief! and people need love!

Drawing the first cover, though *crude* by most standards, was a way for me to solidify my commitment to write "the book". Early on, when Bruce was messin' with me about writing a book, I led him on by saying "ya know, if we ever really do this thing, we're going to call it *"Fake it Til You Make it*!"

However, with the things that were coming down in 2008, it was Michael Graham who was the first person to suggest that I might want to consider a title name change. Bill Peelle, recognizing the times we were in, said "Yeah, you'll probably want to call it *'Fake it Til You Make it... Again!'"*

Well, Bill was right, there wasn't a one of us that had not taken a kick in the teeth emotionally and financially from every direction.

So then we began to play around with other titles, such as: *"Faith it 'til You Make it", "You Don't Mess with God", "Seven Secrets to Success", "Honey, You Don't Understand", "Miracles, Angels and Life", "Life is Good, Life is God", "The Power of Positive Faith"* and *"Never Give Up*!!"

Also for consideration *"Confessions of a Dirt Farmers Son"*; then there was *"Million Dollar Ways"*; but finally it began to take shape when my good friend, Norma Achor, suggested *"Dream Big and Look Up!"* and my comrade for years, Ben Kaplan, felt strong about *"Faith in the Future"*.

· ·

"Did I mention *CRUDE*?"

But in the end, it was my friend, Shawn Long, who said "of all of your daily habits that you have shared with me, of all the things you do to visualize and to establish your goals, the one single thing which has changed my daily outlook, my daily production and the days of my life is the one where you list on your planner of events for the day, where you write with a magic marker in big, capital letters:

EXPECT A MIRACLE!!

After that, Shawn went on to say *"just as you told me happened in your life, there have been many nights at 10pm or so in the evening when I just look up and said "Lord, I don't know how you did that today" OR "Lord, what a day-you take my breath away!" "For Father, there is no other way that these occurrences could have come together today without Your MIRACLES!!"*

DO YOU BELIEVE IN MAGIC

All my life, I felt lazy, no sense of direction, no way out.

On July 19, 1987, my life changed. That was the day my son was born.

Rick Brannon looked into his little boy's eyes and at that moment said "I don't want your life, Ricky, to be like mine."

"I remember being poor all the time; I went to Martinsville elementary school and I knew I was poor just by the way the teachers and other kids looked at me. In the second grade, my principal, Mr. Allen, took me to buy new shoes because my shoes had holes in the side."

" When I was 12, I helped my uncle build his house in Midland; he picked me up everyday afterschool."

"The day Ricky was born, I was 24 years old and unemployed."

"I began working any jobs I could do. For 2 years I worked for Don Thompson Excavating in Spring Valley and I was able to save $4,000."

"With that money, I was able to purchase a garage in New Antioch with my loan payments being $79 per month."

"I went back to my mechanic roots, fixing and repairing cars and trucks in that little garage in New Antioch. With the help of my neighbors and friends, I built a little apartment with two bedrooms inside the garage."

"In 1997 I put my entire life savings into starting a car lot in Reesville, Ohio. It was a big step for me and another huge life changing decision."

"But, wow, the car thing took off and caught on fire with business!"

"We have been totally, totally blessed over the past years!"

"I now have several employees and many rental properties; things are great."

Most recently, Rick teamed up with professional wrestler and actor, Bill Goldberg; through Rick's generousity and the customized re-creation of the 1970 Plymouth Satellite (a replica of the championship racecar Richard Petty drove into history every Sunday in the early 1970's) the car was sold at a charity auction for $501,000!

Rick said, "the car sold in the top 20 money cars; through additional donations, the total contributions from Rick's car alone, reached nearly $700,000!"

Rick said, "Meeting Richard Petty was very cool; he was just a wonderful guy."

MIRACLE, from rags to Hollywood?!

Rick Brannon Sr., owner of Rick's Auto Sales in Reesville, donated the 1970 Plymouth Sattelite to actor and former pro-wrestler, Bill Goldberg, who created the NASCAR Superbird, "No. 43", in honor of Petty, who retired from competitive driving at the end of the 1992 season.

Today, through just an unbelievable work ethic and a true sense of fairness, Rick Brannon has a very busy and exciting life.

Rick Brannon will tell you with tears in his eyes, "things seem well and I'm not the same person I once was."

BLUEPRINT FOR YOUR LIFE

1. Goals should be written on a sheet of paper; otherwise, it is merely a daydream, a wish and it is likely to never happen.

2. Goals must be specific.

3. Goals must be attainable; generally, it is best to break them into 3 month, 6 month, 9 month and 12 months for short-term goals. Long-term goals can be broken down in a period of 5, 10, 15 or even 20 years.

4. Effective goals should be challenging goals. The goal must be so desirous that you are willing to "pay the price"!

5. Set goals in all areas of your life.

It is important not only to reduce your goals to writing, but to also review them <u>daily</u>, <u>weekly</u> and <u>monthly!!</u>

And finally, be specific with a target date; in this case, this little book needs to be published no later than October 15, 2009.

6. Review your goals on a regular basis; many people review them every day; they should be reviewed at least once a week.

7. Goals are subject to change and after the years 2008, 2009 and 2010, who doesn't know that? When your entire savings is down 50% and your income dwindles down, your short-term goals will need to be adjusted as you reach within your soul to pull yourself up out of the hole.

8. I believe, if possible, that a good time to write goals is at the beginning of each year.

9. Just writing your goals, which will develop into a blueprint for your life, is very exciting!

10. Don't be afraid to set goals. It's exciting to reach for the stars!

Prayer, coupled with your goals, is an amazing thing.

Mark 11:24 "Whatever things you desire when you pray, believe that you receive *them*, and you will have *them*."

GOALS IN WRITING

INITIALLY, YOU MAY USE A FORMAT SIMILAR TO THE ONE BELOW:

Goals for 2011

I.   GOD-FAITH

II   FAMILY

III   PROFESSION OR SCHOOL

IV.   FINANCES

V.   SOCIAL

VI.   PHYSICAL

VII.   SHORT-TERM DREAMS (OR SOMETHING PERSONAL TO YOU)

VIII.   LONG-TERM DREAMS (OR SOMETHING PERSONAL TO YOU)

> *J.C. Penney said: "Show me a stockclerk with a goal*
>
> *and I'll show you a man who will make history*
>
> *But show me a man who has no goals*
>
> *And I'll show you a stockclerk!"*

CLASSROOM IN YOUR CAR

Years ago, I ordered Zig Zigler's cassette tapes (CD's in today's world) on both Goal Setting and Personal Achievement.

I would listen to his tapes continuously from the time I got up in the morning, while I was shaving, showering and on my to the office; as a lot of my time during the day is in my automobile, it was also an opportunity to listen to Zig throughout the day!

Being one of literally thousands of whom he has mentored, I, like many others, could finish every sentence that Zig started!

He would say that it takes sixteen times to listen to tape recorded material before it becomes imbedded and becomes a part of you!

Whoever your mentor is, I would highly recommend that you utilize your driving time to receive your morning spiritual message. Whether you listen to Christian music like Michael W Smith or Steven Curtis Chapman, or listen to the great motivational speakers, such as Tony Robbins, Brian Tracey, or, Mr. Zig Zigler, the morning drive is a great time to get pumped up, revitalized and to prepare for a <u>SUPER</u> <u>GOOD</u> <u>DAY</u>!

If you WANT the feeling, LISTEN to the feeling, then you'll HAVE the feeling!

SELF TALKS

There are many go-getters, successful business and salespeople who actually incorporate their goals and positive affirmation into "SELF-TALK". Most goal-setters will repeat out loud their written affirmation at least once a day. If they've written their goals by the first of the year, many achievers will have them memorized by the end of January.

Tommy Hopkins, the well-known sales trainer from Scottsdale, Arizona, has shared a great motivator self talk to assist being prepared for the day. Many times, after I have affirmed my self talk on my way to the office, I will follow-up with Tommy's motivating words as I drive the car to the office parking lot. I give Tommy all the credit, but if you're just getting started into visualizing success, preparing for the next level, this is a great way to get started!

NOTE: I challenge you to memorize these words and just before you walk into the front door of your school building, before you walk into your first college class of the day, or just before you walk into your office or your place of business, lift yourself up to your *next energy level* with the *enthusiasm of these words*!!

You'll be pumped up, ready to produce, ready to be the WINNER that you are, ready to be a GREAT ONE as you walk into your venue in the morning hours!!

■■

I will win.

Why? I'll tell you why!

Because I have faith, courage and enthusiasm.

Today, I'll meet the right people at the right place at the right time for the betterment of all.

I see opportunity in every challenge.

I'm terrific at remembering names and faces.

When I fail, I only look at what I did right.

I never take advice from anyone more messed up than I am.

I only let positive thoughts enter my mind.

I am a winner, a contributor, an achiever, I believe in me!

I'm alive, I'm awake and I feel great!!

I feel good, I feel fine, I feel this way all the time!!

Tommy Hopkins

SMILE A LITTLE SMILE

> *Several years ago, a study at Yale University revealed something that good sales people have known for a long time. After weeks of testing appearances and attitudes of people, the professors at Yale discovered that a smile is the <u>single</u> <u>most</u> <u>powerful</u> <u>force</u> of <u>influence</u> that we have. A warm, friendly smile shows you are open, shows you are easy to be around and in general, some smiles even show the depth of your soul.*

For years, on-my-way-to-work self talks, I always had near the beginning:

SMILE!

SMILE!

Not being the "brightest bulb in the hall" in the early hours of the day, I need to remind myself to "be up", "be on" (that means *be alert* for anything today which might pass you by if you're not "on your game") and SMILE! Even on the phone, I make every effort to put on a SMILE...

My friend, financial advisor, Phil Snow, has a great smile!

He's the kind of a guy that can walk into a room and fill up the whole room with light; there are other people that can *brighten* up a whole room just by *walking* out of it!

Jonda Towner, who runs our office, has two great sons- both of her sons, Timmy and Jeremy, have infectious smiles!

My friend, Congressman Bob McEwen has a great smile!

I'm not talking about an insincere grin; being plastic doesn't fool anybody; folks can tell when it's put on. I am talking about a real smile, one that comes from within; the kind of heartwarming smile that will lift you up to the next level in business, sales and LIFE!

Nancy LaRocca, who handles our advertising, has a terrific smile- one that just keeps on giving!

Mindy McCarty-Stewart, principal of Mason High School, has an incredibly beautiful smile!

Marsha Bennett, of the Bennett Real Estate Company, has a genuine, caring and sparkling smile!

President John F. Kennedy had a stunning smile!

President Ronald Reagan had an inviting, contagious smile!

President Barack Obama has an absolutely sincere open smile!

Isn't it amazing how all these charismatic people have smiles that invite you into their soul, into their spirit, into their being!

SMILE!

SMILE!

▪▪

HERE COMES THE SUN

One of the kindest people I know is Nikki.

And what a <u>SMILE</u>!

Nikki Haines is a server at Damon's Grill in Wilmington for the lunch crowd.

Over the years, our friends, David and Cindy Camp have provided great service and excellent food at this popular local eatery; the noon servers, Susan, Sherry, Angie and Jimmy are most professional!

During lunch one day, while Nikki was in the vicinity of our table, my guest and Nikki were talking about prayer. She said, "I've always prayed since I was a little girl; in fact, you're going to think I'm crazy, but I know I've always had angels around me; many angels. Angels have watched over and protected me all of my life."

In fact, she said, "sometimes when I know that someone is in need, perhaps my Mom, sometimes a friend, I'll just say to my angels, "you go and take care of them for awhile; I'll be ok."

She said, "You know, I even prayed for God to give me the right person to be my husband" and she said with her big smile, " and God gave me Todd!"

She and Todd have been married for several years, have two great sons, Kameron and Noah, and they have a wonderful life.

But it's her *beautiful, natural smile* that allows you to peer deep into her soul.

That's Nikki.

> *Some of us are not blessed with natural, radiant smiles, like Nikki; sometimes we have to remind ourselves to "be on"!*

One day I stopped by to visit my friend, Ron Trustee, at his insurance firm. After entering his office, he leaped up from his chair, nearly jumped over his desk to welcome me with a big, broad smile and shouted out "How ya doin' today?" Nothing that Ron did was put on; when you have that kind of sincere persona and you are that happy to greet customers in your office, it makes for great business!

For as my friend, Ron, exemplifies, "People do not care how much *you know*, until they know how much *you care!*"

To show that you care, why not start off with a sincere smile.

HOW GREAT THOU ART

Coming from a modest background is my friend, Shawn Long.

Even though in high school he was a very good athlete, at times because of his "defenses" (that many of us have at that age) he would sometimes allow himself to get out of control.

I watched Shawn over the past years develop slowly, inch by inch, in a very positive way.

When Shawn was 21 years old he asked to visit with me; at the time he said he needed $500 for a business opportunity. I gave him the money and never thought much about it.

That particular business "opportunity" did not work out.

As a kid, he, like myself, had few material things, but he and his brothers and sister did have a Dad and Mom who loved them and always took pride in what their children were doing.

Shawn, in the past six years has developed his own system of buying homes and either renting them or flipping them; he is a diligent worker and a kid who has pulled himself up from the rough times; I have also admired how Shawn has unselfishly lifted up those around him.

About four years ago, he encouraged his brother, Joe, to be involved in the real estate business. Like Shawn did in the beginning, Joe is still treading water.

Today Shawn and Joe are on equal footing and they have formed a partnership. Recently, the two brothers acquired a Wilmington downtown store front to conduct their realty business activities.

An interesting aside about Shawn Long is that three Christmas's ago he asked me to stop by his home while his wife Sara was away at a holiday party.

Well, it wasn't just a stop-by!

Shawn presented me with a brand new set of Tony Robbins' tapes (apparently I had given him my own set at one time), and yes, presented me the $500 from many years ago.

As I left his and Sara's beautiful home that evening, we both had tears in our eyes.

We both recognized that Shawn's goal-setting, coupled with prayer and faith, had thrusted him into this position of success at a young age.

Zig says, "You go as far as you can see;

and then when you get there, you can see further!"

WE ALL HAVE SKEPTICS

There will be skeptics that say this little book with no more depth than this, without using any more than four syllable words, that a book of this simplicity can not begin to bring young people, people of all ages further along in their confidence level of "Yes I Can Do It"!

You are welcome to stay as you are. And if you are happy as you are, please never change!

I'm not asking anyone to "change their personality; I'm only suggesting if your goal in life is to be more-is to be the most you can be, that carefully watching others traits who are enjoying a positive amount of good fortune, who are involved in strong success, that these are traits that you might want to observe closely and adopt according to how they can be structured within you.

Because I believe, that this is no different, than hundreds of amateur golfers watching Tiger Woods every move, from the graceful flow of his back swing to produce his powerful 325 yard drives, to the finesse' touch as he works through the texture of the bunkers and the stunning results of his thousands of hours of practice putting from all surfaces in all conditions.

Or, for that matter, how many young basketball players today have learned to adopt the LeBron move as he focuses toward the bucket, cups the basketball within his chest so as to make it difficult for the defender to take a swipe at the ball, so that when he gets toward the goal, he has the opportunity to score from several different angles and dunks, all of which he has practiced and worked on *thousands of times* prior to the shot he takes in the game winning seconds!

If you're going to improve a step at a time toward your goals of success, you must learn by watching others who have attained the high level of success which you *see in your mind's eye*.

If you want to hit a fast ball coming in at 96 miles per hour then you'll need to grab the bat, take instruction, take additional lessons from hitting coaches and make sure that you *work* two hours a day with balls coming at you, using your wrists for power. Then you'll have the gumption, then you'll have the guts, then you'll have the glory, then you'll have the fruits of your labor; then someday you'll be in the *BIGS*, but only if you work, work, work!!!

Sometimes I hear high school football players and basketball players say they are going to practice; and for these young men it is *just* a practice; but for those *athletes* who have a *burning desire* within them to be great, it is not *just a practice*; it is two hours of *working your butt off, sweating your tail end off; doing more, staying longer, being the best*!!

. . . .

And now, starting at guard, at 6' from *Lees Creek, Ohio*, BOBBY HOOPER!!

With the possible exception of Pete Rose, I know of no one from this area in recent memory who had more guts, more determination, more competitiveness and more confidence as an athlete.

In Bobby Hooper's case, he could have played in the BIGS, had he made that decision; in his sophomore year, as a Dayton basketball legend, he was approached by the Pittsburg Pirates who wanted to sign the short-stop to a professional contract.

"They had a dozen Louisville slugger bats with them" said Hooper, "the bats had my name on them! That was a tough decision at the time!"

Bobby Hooper, who had played both basketball and baseball at the University of Dayton as a freshman and sophomore would ultimately have to give up baseball because of the success and length of the basketball seasons. Going deep into the basketball season with the Flyers, Bobby was unavailable for baseball until a month into the season.

As Bobby was completing his high school career at Simon-Kenton in Lees Creek, his mailbox was full of baseball and basketball offers from all over the country; he visited several NCAA Division I schools; he said "Don Donaher, (who he affectionately refers to as 'Mick') simply said to him 'if you come, I'll give you a fair chance, like I do all the other kids; but I can promise, you'll get an education.' "

Bobby said "he didn't blow any smoke, he was straight-forward and I liked him immediately".

Bobby said in the locker room, Coach Donaher would say "We have to be prepared together and individually, *mentally, physically, spiritually*."

A 6'0" guard, Bobby was a starter from his very first varsity game and was a leader on teams that reached the NCAA sweet-16 his sophomore season, the NCAA Championship game his junior year and the 1968 NIT Championship his senior year.

It was in 1967, his junior year, that Bobby Hooper hit a 25-foot game winning basket in the first round of the NCAA Tournament to lift the Flyers to a 69-67 overtime win over Western Kentucky.

"THE SHOT" to win over Western Kentucky.

The following game, the University of Dayton upset #3 in the country Tennessee, 53-52; then in the "elite 8" beat Virginia Tech in overtime, 66-63.

In the final-four classic, UD went on to upset the #2 team in the nation, North Carolina (coached by Dean Smith) 76-62.

Just days later, Hooper, Donny May and company went on to meet John Wooden's unbeaten UCLA Bruins (headlined by Lou Alcinder aka Kareem Abdul Jabbar) for the Championship; they lost that final game, but UD won the hearts as the Cinderella team of the country!

Bobby said in those days his competitive nature was such that if the other team was going to win, they were going to have to **beat him up**, because he was going after *"every loose ball, make every free throw, make every defensive stop necessary, rebound at both ends and make the play necessary to win the game!"*

In 1968, Bobby's senior year, U.D. beat JoJo White's Kansas team for the NIT Championship. Bobby went on to play with the Indiana Pacers, but having broken his hand during Dayton's Championship in 1968, he re-broke the same hand with the Pacers in '69 and then broke the same hand for a third time. Bobby's playing days were over.

Though our area has had many skilled athletes and legends, I know of no one who has played at the professional basketball level other than Bobby Joe Hooper. Bobby said those years with Donaher's Dayton Flyers were wonderful; because of Donaher's philosophy it brought him closer to the Lord.

Even today, Bobby says I live by the same philosophy I learned from "Mick" Donaher years ago:

1. Pray
2. Plan
3. Focus
4. Finish

I remember Bobby Joe Hooper playing for the University of Dayton; I remember thinking this guy has the heart of a tiger! Here is a guy I'd like my grandkids to emulate.

Bobby Hooper <u>NEVER</u> <u>GAVE</u> <u>UP</u>!!

SECTION V

Wilmington, Ohio
6000 Air Park Jobs Lost
May 29, 2008

WILMINGTON News Journal

Thursday, May 29, 2008   Serving Clinton County, Ohio, since 1838   50 CENTS

6,000 air park jobs to be lost

WILMINGTON

DHL to partner with UPS

By GARY HUFFENBERGER
ghuffenberger@wnewsj.com

The parent company of DHL said Wednesday it will change to a new partner for its air shipments within North America, a move that's expected to mean the loss of about 6,000 to 6,100 ABX Air jobs in Wilmington.

The planned deal between DHL and UPS also is expected to have a major impact upon ASTAR Air Cargo. ASTAR and ABX are DHL's current air carriers for the shipments UPS will transport in the future. ASTAR has hundreds of employees based at the DHL Air Park in Wilmington.

ABX Air's night sort operations will be eliminated because the night sort serves, and is served by, the air cargo network whose function will be performed by UPS, said ABX Air President John Graber.

Graber on Wednesday said it

Graber

was "a grim day for ABX Air, frankly for the Wilmington community, for the county, for the state."

The ABX president added, "This is going to be really hard on thousands of employees and thousands more family members, and people in the community."

"We tried to talk about this openly, honestly and face-to-face with our employees, and tell them that none of them deserve it. And that it's a really, really hard thing to go through and we'll help each other get through it," Graber said late Wednesday afternoon.

At a press conference in the Bonn, Germany headquarters of Deutsche Post World Net (DPWN), which is DHL's parent company, DPWN Chief Executive Officer Frank Appel said the restructuring of DHL's business in the United States involved a "comprehensive and radical plan."

The U.S. division of DHL has been losing hundreds of millions of dollars annually. DHL Express CEO John Mullen, at the Bonn press conference, called it DPWN's "biggest problem by far."

The changes entailed in the restructuring plan, said Mullen, show that DPWN is prepared "to take radical and decisive action" to make U.S. operations viable.

When the restructuring has

See JOBS, Page 3A

WILMINGTON News Journal

Friday, July 11, 2008   Serving Clinton County, Ohio, since 1838   50 CENTS

DHL brought before McCain

PORTSMOUTH

Mary Houghtaling speaks out

By BRANDON SMITH
bsmith@wnewsj.com

The voice of Wilmington's Mary Houghtaling was heard across the nation on a public news radio show Thursday morning — she got the chance Wednesday to ask John McCain about DHL.

McCain, who held a town-hall meeting in Portsmouth, has been reported by the Associated Press and Time magazine's website as giving Houghtaling a "straight" answer.

Houghtaling herself thinks so, too.

"He was as honest as he could be," said the Hospice co-founder and DHL advocacy leader. "I thought he was very gracious and he seemed very sympathetic. ... He didn't blow any smoke, or give any false hope."

"This is a terrible blow," said the Senator in response to her questioning.

But he soon gave the part of the speech for which he's getting the most national media attention.

"I would be glad to ask for any investigation or, uh, scrutiny, of what DHL is doing, okay?" said McCain.

"Mm-hmm," Houghtaling uttered into the microphone.

"But I gotta look you into the eye and give you straight talk. I don't know if I can stop it or not. Or, if it will be stopped," he said.

The Senator then spoke for another two minutes on his plans to increase the effectiveness of job training.

Houghtaling, a supporter of McCain, nevertheless concedes that like other politicians, he uses just about every

See McCAIN, Page 2A

STUNNING DHL ANNOUNCEMENT HITS COMMUNITY HARD

Wendell Willkie said "I believe in America because in America we are free, because we dream great dreams and because we have the opportunity to make those dreams come true."

In the summer of 2008, many decent hardworking people in southwestern Ohio saw their "American dream" come to a screeching halt. Not one single person outside of the few upper level decision makers at ABX foresaw this travesty coming.

For many families, it was the beginning of a painful, financially hurtful and devastating process, with no light at the end of the tunnel. As the weeks went on, it was apparent that for any help to come, this infamous massacre was going to have to reach the White House if it were to attain national exposure.

Mary Houghtaling was the first area citizen to initiate such high profile exposure. On June 9, 2008, at Presidential candidate John McCain's town meeting in Portsmouth, Ohio, Mary Houghtaling drove the distance and made a gutsy delivery as she questioned Senator McCain by asking "What are you going to do about the DHL disaster?"

Senator McCain apparently was shocked. He said he wasn't aware of anything like that going on. He couldn't promise anything, but he would look into it.

Four days later, June 13, the exchange between Mary and Senator McCain hit the front page of the Sunday edition of the Cleveland Plain Dealer! While this was going on, Bruce McKee, an ABX employee announced "it is not important to me what political party or group can help solve this disaster. In my opinion, it is necessary to find help <u>somewhere</u>, as soon <u>as</u> <u>possible</u> <u>from</u> <u>someone</u>." He decided he would seek <u>all options.</u>

WILMINGTON
News Journal

Wednesday, July 16, 2008   Serving Clinton County, Ohio, since 1826   50 CENTS

ABX persists with bid overtures

WILMINGTON

ABX president lauds overtures

News Journal staff report

(article text)

Other on Monday five underscored half proud for a of the Wilmington ABX employees who preferred on the job since DHL.

> "We remain convinced DHL and its customers would be better served by our dedicated, efficient and customized air network in the United States."
> — John Graber, ABX Air president

Obama briefed on air park

U.S. Sen. Barack Obama, the presumptive Democratic nominee for president, was Friday for a briefing on the situation at the Wilmington Air Park. When asked to come to Wilmington, Obama told ABX Air employees Bryan McKay.

That is why he organized a meeting with the Obama people. This meeting lasted well over two hours in the lower level of our real estate office.

On July 11 , Wilmington Mayor Raizk, Bruce McKee and a handful of other officials, spent one on one facetime with Presidential Candidate Barack Obama. That morning, in Dayton, Ohio, Barack Obama altered his entire speech and brought to the forefront of the nation the DHL derailment that was occurring in Wilmington, Ohio.

Within days, Mary Houghtaling had arranged to have a preliminary meeting with two John McCain staffers. I was invited to attend; after listening for twenty minutes, it did not appear to me that this meeting was providing any momentum toward getting the Senator to Wilmington.

The little McCain puppets at the end of the table were politely smiling; I felt they were more about where they would have lunch than the crisis at hand. I was leaving the General Denver Hotel meeting and began to head to my car. Halfway out, Mary Houghtaling yelled after me, "You've got to say something!"

I really wasn't in the mood to say something, but I didn't want to let her down. I went back with Mary, she interrupted the meeting and asked those in attendance to listen to what I had to say.

I looked at the McCain puppets and said "You people don't get it! John McCain doesn't get it! John McCain is shaking hands with three dozen people at a coffeehouse in Columbus, less than 50 minutes away from the most important hotbed in the country, and he doesn't appear to know how important this crisis is!"

Looking at the puppets again, I said "you're sitting here not taking anything too serious. You have no clue of the devastation, the hurt, and the financial woes that thousands in this area are going through. If you don't get off your butts and tell McCain that he just doesn't get it, then he has no chance whatsoever; he needs to get his butt down here and see for himself the injustice that is occurring against 10,000 people!"

I was done. I was through. I turned back on my heels, headed down the hall and walked out the General Denver front door.

As I got in my car, I figured I had done as much damage as I could do. Fortunately, I later found out that this was a catalyst to open up the line of communication with the John McCain people.

Within 48 hours, Mary Houghtaling had her answer.

McCain had agreed to a private meeting with 24 representatives in the area, squeezing this Wilmington stop in between a northern Ohio rally and a Clermont County fundraiser. This meeting was scheduled at 2pm on August 7th, at the Kelly Center at Wilmington College.

By now, the stakes had been lifted higher for both presidential candidates. It appeared to many that Wilmington and the ten surrounding counties could <u>actually</u> <u>determine</u> this presidential election!

On the day of Senator McCain's arrival, approximately 250 ABX/DHL/Astar employees and representatives stood some 50 yards away from the Kelly Center entrance on the Wilmington College campus, hoping to get a glimpse of the Senator before he left town. The only people in the tension-filled room were the 24 invitees as well as some national reporters of networks and publications. There were a number of higher echelon ABX/DHL/Astar folks in the room who had greater knowledge than I. I vowed it was my job to <u>SHUT-UP</u> and <u>LISTEN</u>!

After the 45 minute closed session, Senator McCain held a brief press conference in a small room off the hallway leading from the Kelly Center.

My friend, Bruce McKee, was in the hallway and said to me "we've got to get him outside to see these people." I said, "Bruce, you're absolutely right, he *cannot* leave here without giving these folks a ray of hope."

Within seconds of that conversation, John McCain headed down the narrow hallway towards us, alone, without anyone near him. Bruce grabbed his right arm and I was on his left.

I started pouring my heart out into Senator's McCain ear, I said "Sir, you must come with us, come see these people and give them hope, for they have been standing out here in the hot, blazing sun for the past two hours. They need to see that you care about them."

He looked over at Bruce and asked "Is it O.K.?" His implication was "will it be safe?" Bruce, who had already had a chance to visit with many of the folks waiting outside, said "Senator, you'll be fine."   The tension was continuing to mount as we headed out to the yellow tape, holding back the bystanders.

As we walked briskly towards the most dedicated workers in southwestern Ohio, I continued to exchange information with the Senator, mostly, "Sir, you must raise the spirits of these people; you must give them a reason for living; you must give them hope. They are down-trodden, they are hurting, they are beat up, financially broke and they know it! Please, please give them love and give them hope!"

WILMINGTON
News Journal

Friday, August 8, 2008   Serving Clinton County, Ohio, since 1826   50 CENTS

'We have an ally'

McCain visits Wilmington to hear community concerns over DHL deal

WILMINGTON

By GARY HUFFENBERGER
ghuffenberger@wnewsj.com

"We have an ally in John McCain ... we have an ally."

— Joe Truchori, an ABTAR Air Cargo pilot who has been instrumental in the Save the Jobs campaign, following the meeting Thursday at Wilmington College with Sen. John McCain.

Above, McCain poses for a photo with Mary Haughtaling. McCain reached Haughtaling with inspiring his visit. Below, residents don T-shirts and carry signs hoping McCain will "feel our pain."

See McCAIN, Page 14A

McCain
FEEL OUR
PAIN

DHL - UPS
Destroying   Anti-Trust
Homes &   Anti-American
Lives   Anti-Worker
www.savethejobs.org

Turner calls McCain
a powerful senator

On that day, Senator John McCain was well-received. They were happy to see him. They were happy that he was in Wilmington. They were happy that he cared enough to be there that day!

Countless other meetings had been held in the preceding months. Through Mayor Raizk, a task force had been formed. In addition, Senator Sherrod Brown, Congressman Mike Turner, Commissioners Mike Curry, Randy Riley, David Stewart and other community leaders, worked diligently to improve the area job environment.

From May 29, 2008, there was a season of struggle, pain, hurt and financial loss for the folks and businesses suffering from the ripple effect throughout Clinton County and the surrounding southwestern Ohio area.

CHRISTMAS 2008

December 21, 2008

Bible Missionary Baptist Church
Wilmington, Ohio

These are the introductory words of Pastor Kurtis Summerville's message the Sunday before Christmas 2008: "...*this Christmas has been a unique Christmas, but not the worst. This Christmas has been a unique Christmas in the fact that we are standing at the precipice of great loss. But I want you to know today, even at the precipice of great loss, God has a remedy.*

God has a remedy for our recession. I need to take you back 10 years ago. Ten years ago, I was asked to be pastor of this church, 10 years ago this month. And on a Sunday 10 years ago, I remember my wife walking into church using a cane, her back had been bothering her and we had tried all kinds of remedies with the doctors and the doctors kept saying 'we've got it figured out' but things kept getting worse. I'll never forget that by the time we had our Sunday night service, she was using a walker to get out of the church. Her ability to walk had degraded that much.

But in a time of recession, in our personal lives, we saw the Lord step in. I'll never forget the fact that by that Monday morning, she was in the hospital. In the hospital not able to walk and on Christmas Eve, they did 13 hours of surgery and when she came out they said 'she might not be able to walk'. But then, I remember when the surgeon was talking, I said 'but God's got things under control'.

Stand up, stand up, baby, that's her walking, that's her able to stand when the doctors didn't think she would make it. And I'm here to tell you, in the midst of a recession, in the midst of our bad times, the pundits may say 'we will not make it', the pundits may say 'it will not work', but we have a God we can trust. We have a God that we can trust that can get you through.

God has a remedy. Yeah, things look bad, but God has a remedy. I remember 10 years ago, things looked bad; <u>the same God that gave my wife the ability to walk, the same God that guided the surgeon's hands, the same God that helped the surgeon tweeze her bone from her spinal cord, the same God is the same God that is here right now, in Wilmington, Ohio. He has a remedy for our recession</u>.

I don't know about you, but I'm glad I serve a God who has a remedy for my bad times.

If you'll peruse the parameters of this text with me, I just want to share a few things. One thing I want you to know. Recessions have many labels. You can call it whatever you want; you can call it a famine, you can call it a shortage, you can call it a time of bitterness, you can call it a layoff, you can call it a shutdown, you can call it a time of market correction, but I want you to know, whatever you call it, it has the same results. <u>You don't have enough money to pay the bills</u>..."

WHEN YOU WALK THROUGH A STORM,
KEEP YOUR HEAD UP HIGH

"I just couldn't take it anymore; in the pouring rain, I pulled over to the side of US 35 heading to Dayton and just began to bawl".

"It had been bottled in; for over fifteen minutes, I cried and I hurt so much".

I said, "God, I can't do this".

"I can't make it".

"Lord, if you want me to throw up my hands and give up, just say so".

"My wife is in the hospital, she's had a thirteen hour operation and she is still unable to walk; I've got three kids whom I love; I just can't do it anymore by myself".

"I have a son who has severe disabilities, but we're going to make it".

"I have just been named Pastor less than three weeks ago at our church".

"I know you say, you don't put anymore on us than what we can bear".

"I know that's what you say".

It was at that moment, that Pastor Kurtis Summerville recalled, the Lord spoke to me in a way in which I shall never forget:

"COUNT IT ALL JOY WHEN YOU FALL".

Today, Kurtis Summerville, Pastor of the Wilmington Missionary Baptist Church continues to deliver spell-bounding, passionate, deep-faith teachings every Sunday morning. He has never forgot what the Lord told him on what was, perhaps, the most difficult few days of his life.

"COUNT IT ALL JOY WHEN YOU FALL".

Kurtis Summerville grew up in Camden, New Jersey, one of three children, with a mother who he has described as wise, selfless, and filled with love for her three children.

There were many times, he has said, that the kitchen cupboard was almost bare. Nonetheless, his mother worked hard to improve their lives. Somehow, between her regular job and childrearing, she found the time to earn her undergraduate degree from Rutgers University and later a Master's degree as well.

Kurtis says his Mother stressed, *"Don't have a ghetto mentality!"*

She encouraged her children to do three things:
1. pray
2. work hard

and 3. get an education.

Today, Kurtis' older brother Tom is an attorney in Philadelphia. His younger sister, Tonya, teaches English in Spain.

From the ghetto of Camden, New Jersey, where you live in a "crisis mode" every time you walk down the street, Kurtis Summerville said a family friend encouraged him to consider Cedarville College in Cedarville, Ohio.

He said, "*I knew at the age of 5 that I would be a preacher.*"

Today, Kurtis Summerville is a well-known mentor and teacher of other pastors throughout the United States, and has preached to congregations as large as 15,000 in Phoenix, Los Angeles, Dallas, Houston and London, England.

Kurtis would be the first to tell you that he is blessed in a million different ways. Along with his beautiful and talented wife Denise, three great kids, Alyssa, Daniel and Jordan, and a terrific, loving, spirited congregation in Wilmington, Ohio.

It seems like a hundred years ago, but he has never forgotten that dark, dreary night on the side of the road. Kurtis Summerville wiped the tears from his eyes, drove to the hospital and says, "*I've been fine ever since*".

"COUNT IT ALL JOY WHEN YOU FALL"

* * *

LAUGHTER IN THE RAIN

In May, 2009, comedian Jay Leno, of the "Tonight Show", flew in from Los Angeles; he delivered two outstanding performances telling jokes in rapid, express-delivery fashion! At the close of his show, he remarked he had seen news reports about the Wilmington area and on those reports, he had not seen much complaining. Rather, he went on to say, he saw lots of decent people who really got screwed! This was his closing on both performances and drew huge applause, largely comprised of workers who had been laid off.

In spite of the limited employment opportunities, the faith of the people in this community seems to deepen. Many are figuring out ways to stay in a community they have grown to love... for its schools and so much more.

But lastly, it's the gutsy fiber make-up of the folks who reside in southwestern Ohio; it's the deep faith where they count on the Lord; as Paul said *"my God shall supply all your needs, according to His riches in Glory, by Christ Jesus"*.

∎∎

"I WILL PREPARE MYSELF AND SOME DAY MY OPPORTUNITY WILL COME." ~ Abraham Lincoln

He was born the last of seven children. That's probably interesting enough. He figured out, when he was old enough to figure it out, that the older six children always got to sleep in the best parts of the attic. The first floor of the little shack in which his family lived was their total living and eating space.

I bet there were times that he had his ankles and arms intertwined with his brothers and sisters most of the night!

When he got to be three or four or five, and still the youngest, he began to notice that at supper time, there's not much food to *begin with,* and, unless you're quick, there's not any food to *end with*.

Someone who I greatly admire lived in this modest shanty (did I mention it had a dirt floor) at the dead end of Thorne Avenue in Wilmington. The dirt floor was so clean, he recalls, that he never really noticed the make-up of the flooring.

Fortunately, for Bruce McKee, his way out and his way up was football.

As a star athlete on the Wilmington Hurryin' Hurricane football team, Bruce's confidence and stature begin to grow.

He was captain of a group of kids who went 10-0 his final year at Phoenix Junior College in Arizona. He spent his last couple of years at the University of Louisville.

Bruce and his wife, Vanessa, moved back to Wilmington and have five terrific kids who are high, goal-orientated worker bees.

However, Bruce McKee has fought many battles; some with real estate, some with ABX and many during the situation when DHL

deserted southwestern Ohio and left thousands of workers jobless.

As a leader, Bruce McKee understood what some folks did not; that it was not important what political party or group could help solve this disaster; it was just important to find *help somewhere, as soon as possible, from someone!*

He decided he would seek all options; that is why, early on, Bruce McKee organized a meeting with the Obama people.

The meeting lasted well over two hours in the lower level of our real estate office.

Within days, along with Wilmington Mayor Raizk and a handful of other officials, Bruce McKee spent one-on-one time with then presidential candidate Barrack Obama.

That morning in Dayton, Ohio, Barrack Obama altered his entire speech by bringing to the forefront of the nation the DHL train derailment that was occurring in Wilmington, Ohio.

Bruce McKee was one of only a handful who had actual face-to-face time with both presidential candidates!

Along the way, he was asked to be involved in commercials for Congressman Mike Turner. He appeared on a segment of "60 minutes" regarding the DHL debacle in late January, 2009.

Listening very carefully to others before offering his opinion is what has made Bruce McKee a most respected leader in the Wilmington community.

Bruce McKee will continue to be visible as a community representative and one whose time has come!

And now, as time passes, only a few visible reminders remain. Walking quietly down the street of our little town is a journalist by the name of Bryan Mealer who arrived in Wilmington in May 2009 to begin research on a book about the impact of the DHL layoffs. In New York City where he resides, Bryan Mealer would be noticed in many venues as he is a former Associated Press staff writer and respected international journalist. However, in our little city, he is barely noticed as he quietly goes about his job.

So, nearly a year and a half after that stunning headline, normalcy is slowly returning. The sun is beginning to shine brighter over the city of Wilmington and the surrounding area.

A few years ago, a Wilmington Chamber of Commerce slogan stated: **"In Wilmington, It's the People!"**

Even more importantly, TODAY…

"It's *still* the People!"

SECTION VI

Depression is a Killer

BLUER THAN BLUE

I believe that all of us, at one time or another, has a "down" time; sometimes it lasts for a week, sometimes a month, sometimes it even lasts longer.

In my view, the best way to avoid the "down" days is to work at being "up".

I believe the closer the relationship we have with our heavenly Father, the more of a chance that we will have a *positive way* about us.

I believe the ages from 18-25 years are the most difficult for most any person to work through. This is generally an age of uncertainty, an age of questions, an age of our early loves and an age where we can suffer from deep hurts.

> *An article published by the Washington AP in May, 2009 headlined "Students Stressed, Some Depressed at College". This article related that 85% of the students reported feeling stress in their daily lives with worries about grades, money and relationships being the biggest culprits.*
>
> *At the same time, 42% said they had felt down, depressed or hopeless for several days during the last few weeks.*
>
> *These students complained of trouble sleeping, having little energy and feeling down or hopeless- and most hadn't gotten professional help.*
>
> *Eleven percent said they had thoughts that they would be better off dead.*

That's why I believe the ages between 18 and 25 are the toughest; that's why depression is a killer!

If you are a Christian and have accepted Jesus as your Lord and Savior, then you know you do not walk alone; just by Him being on your right side will help you get through some times that would be most difficult without Him.

■■■

WHAT'S GOING ON

For many of you, you may be going through your first "LIFE-TEST".

Junior-High Students, high school students, college students and young people of all ages, please, please, please read these words!!!

If you are currently going through a down-time, or have a feeling that you have little self-worth, please pray in the morning, during the day and in the evening asking God to get you through this test He has put in front of you.

This is only a "LIFE-TEST"; you will go through more than one "LIFE-TEST". If this is your first one, you may feel like this is the end of the world. You may feel like the world would be better off if you weren't even on the face of it. You don't even want to wake up in the morning. You don't want to get out of bed in the morning. You pull the covers over your head in the morning. You flip over and want to go back to sleep and never wake up.

Unfortunately, this is a natural thing that we go through in life. Does it sting? Absolutely. Will you get through it? Yes, you will!

■■■

SHOW ME THE WAY

There is <u>one</u> person on the face of this Earth that you <u>love</u> <u>the</u> <u>most</u>; whom you <u>trust</u> <u>more</u> <u>than</u> <u>any</u> <u>other</u>, and who <u>will</u> <u>not</u> <u>judge</u> <u>you</u>.

That person may be a parent, your grandmother, your favorite uncle, or your best friend from high school. Go visit that person!! Even if it means taking time off work, school, taking time off, whatever… go spend time with that person that you love and that you trust more than anyone else.

And yes, some of you are going to have your hearts shattered, broken into a million pieces. The hurt is so deep and the knots in your stomach are so big, I don't even have the words to describe it.

• •

IT'S THE DARKEST BEFORE THE DAWN

I can tell you, this "LIFE-TEST" is only temporary; it may last one year, two years, or even longer. The good news is, upon successfully completing God's "LIFE-TEST" for you, you will enter into a period of extreme brightness, cheer, happiness, love and contentment for the next phase of your life.

In fact, thank God if your test is long.

For the longer the duration of your "LIFE-TEST", the brighter and longer will be the NEXT PHASE OF YOUR LIFE!

SOMEWHERE OVER THE RAINBOW

There was this little girl.

This little blue eyed girl was born in a little town in West Germany.

On Saturdays, at the age of 9, this little girl with her younger brother and sister would clean the cobblestone streets of her little town with brooms and dust pans.

The three of them earned $1.25 a week, total, which they diligently gave to their parents to help keep the family afloat.

When this pretty girl was 19, she came to America with her new GI husband, and two little girls in diapers, one in *each arm*.

Six months after her arrival, her GI deserted her.

Penniless, with her two babies, and unable to speak a word of the English language, she continued living in military housing at Fort Carson, Colorado.

A year later, her GI husband returned, promised to stay with her and they moved to his hometown in southern Ohio.

A year later, he was gone; this time for good.

The relocation turned out to be a blessing as she began to learn the English language. With the help of her mother-in-law, using the *TV Guide* as a text, the first two English words she ever read were "General Hospital".

Eventually, Edith got a job at the Blue Grass Restaurant on the south end of Wilmington (today, the location of Blake's Smorgasboard.). Every afternoon, she and her two young daughters walked from their A Street home in the north end of town to the restaurant at the opposite end. She worked nights, earning 50 cents an hour plus tips. Then the three of them would make the long, lonely haul back across town at 2:00 a.m.

Edith's blue eyes shine as she tells you, it was the tips then and the tips today, that have allowed her to put food on the table, clothes on her two girls and buy them the few extras which they were to enjoy. Today, Edith is an established beautician in Wilmington.

A few years ago Edith was on her way out of the shop late on a Saturday afternoon.

A young man knocked on the glass door and sheepishly asked if she could give him a haircut.

Edith said, "I was bone-tired, but this boy was so sincere."

He apologized for making such a last minute request, but explained that he was getting married that very night.

"I didn't charge him for that haircut;" then in her special accent, she told him, "I'll charge you double next time!"

That young man has since sent Edith over twenty of his friends who have been regular customers of hers since that day.

As a little girl in West Germany, she was often told "America is the Land of Dreams!"

Edith has said several times, "I just don't understand it- people here live in the greatest country in the world and they just take it so much for granted- all you have to do is *work* and *give a little of yourself* and *the world can be yours.*"

For Edith, every day she is a free woman in a free country able to make the decisions for herself and do what she wants to do.

No longer is she the little girl in West Germany *sweeping dung off the cobble stone streets of her little town.*

STAYIN' ALIVE

It was a few months ago when my friend, Shelby Bandy, called me and asked me "Are you really going broke?"

I said, "I don't know. Why?"

"Well," she said "I overheard a guy named Joe out at Lowe's telling everyone within voice range, 'I wonder what Butch Peelle is going to do now that he's broke!'" I said, "Shelby, I appreciate you letting me know what's going on."

And then, shortly after, when I was visiting Aunt Dottie; she seemed concerned when she exclaimed that her friend had told her that I had already filed bankruptcy!

DHL's decision to leave was ripping the guts out of southwestern Ohio!

At that point, I knew this was not going to be an easy fix; but this was, indeed, a warning that a "LIFE-TEST" was on its way!

I'd been through two such "LIFE-TESTs" before: the first when I was twenty which lasted for two years; the second was during the 1980, 1981, and 1982 period, when interest rates spiraled up to the 16% to 18% range and no one could afford to buy anything!

During these first two tests, I had grave concerns and those wonderful knots that we all get in our tummy when stress takes over and you wonder if the dark times will ever end.

This time, after going through the first two major tests, and having the comfort that God had brought me through those earlier times, I knew he was holding me in his hand and would bring me through this one!

I believe that God puts us through these tests, to remind us that maybe we have not been thanking Him enough for His favor and the blessings He has showered over us. But as we continue with courage and pray for His guidance, the end results will produce a brighter harvest in our future than we've ever seen!!

This time I simply knew that God would not let me down. Therefore, I wrote on a sheet of paper when I first recognized that we were in trouble:

I'M THROUGH WORRYING

I AM AT PEACE

> *Jesus said, "Peace I give you. Let not your heart be troubled, neither let it be afraid."*

SECTION VII

BITS AND PIECES

DREAMS

Before Madonna ever became an international star, as a little girl, she dreamed and visualized herself being a megastar, being the person she wanted to be, being *MADONNA*!

Henry Ford had a vision; his vision was that he could make the Ford Model-T automobile and be able to sell it at such a price that every family in the country could afford to drive a Ford.

For many that are too young to remember, prior to the affordable automobiles, the only modes of transportation were horseback riding or *walking*; as my good friend Jimmy Connor said *"a bad ride beats a good walk!"*

Henry Ford saw his vision and dream come true!

Barack Obama visualized himself sitting in the oval office years prior to the general election in 2008; long before, he was whispering at the top of his voice "that's [the *White House]* where I'm going to be!"

••

DREAMBOARDS

As I was leaving the classroom after my fifth and final year, I was cleaning out the remaining items in my 8th grade math classroom; one of the remaining items was an old 3X5 bulletin board.

I took it home, hung it up in my little office, and began gradually sticking pictures, articles and other kinds of "things".

Over the past thirty years, I have plastered my entire future, dreams and all, on this board.

Someday, perhaps, I will peel back the pictures and relive my life in reverse.

The pictures that would be found tacked on the original board, would show a picture of a new automobile, a picture of a bigger home, as well as motivational tidbits such as *"How High Would You Reach if You Knew You Couldn't Fail?"*

Other dreams, motivational tidbits and long term goals will be found tacked to the original board.

I highly encourage every human being who has aspirations to becoming the person they want to be, to pick up a bulletin board and begin sticking your goals, your dreams, your future, your ambitions and the people whose traits and stature you admire on the board.

As you grow, over the years, the board transformation will also grow:

1. Early on, the board will contain motivational symbols, quotes, inspirational pictures and short term hopes and aspirations.

2. Next will be the longer term goals such as the luxury automobiles and the new homes and eventually the second resort home or long term dream and goal that you have when you get to a point in life where you can "GO FOR IT!"

3. I think my bulletin board which you see today exemplifies the third stage, that being family, grace, peace, contentment, the people you love and the persons that have inspired you: such as my wife, Dollie, my Father, my Mother, my Father-in-Law, my Brothers, my Daughters, my grandchildren, my son-in-laws; Esther Williams, legendary WHS English teacher; Stan Kellough, who was not only an excellent math teacher, superb realtor but a fine gentleman who was an inspiration to me every time we had a chance to visit; and then there was Ed Loving a renegade who came to Wilmington, turned it upside down, left it a much better place than when he found it; my friend Jerry Rasor, who was on the WLW-C news team out of Columbus for years and a Grand Master of Masons in Ohio; my mentor Zig Ziglar; I have a picture of Johnny Carson, Paul McCartney, Donald Trump, Ronald Reagan, Tommy Hopkins, Dr. Billy Graham and a rally button of Dr. Martin Luther King.

●●●

Your personalized bulletin board will actually come alive over time; it will be a constant three-dimensional reminder that:

You can do what you want to do, be what you want to be and go where you want to go!

"In LIFE, you go as far as you can see and then when you get there, you'll be able to see further!"

BUTCH'S "WALL OF GRATITUDE"

Zig Ziglar, in his offices in Dallas, has, what he calls his "Wall of Gratitude".

Over the years he has encouraged others to do the same.

I took him up on that.

You will see on my "Wall of Gratitude" the following folks who have probably had the most important impact in my formative years and my professional life.

1. The first on the left hand top row is a picture of my parents; my **Mother** who by the time she was fifteen years old had developed a tremendous faith; the kind of person who, even when things were dim, even when things were dark, would give her boys hope and lift up others around her. And my **Father**; who lost his daddy when he was only nine years old (he never seemed to be able to work through that); perhaps that's valid, *but no matter what happens when you're a kid, you've got to put that garbage behind you if you're going to move forward in life!*; my Fathers disciplinarian actions were generally somewhere short of death; on more than one occasion he threatened us boys that "if that happened one more time, he would rub our faces in the bulls poop in the barnyard."
He never did... but it was a scary threat!

2. My grandmother, **Carrie Lundy**; you already know why I loved her so very much!

3. **"Dollie and I"** taken at the Clinton County Fair, thirty days before we were married.

4. My brothers, **Bill and Bob**; I am so proud of both of them; no matter what is going on in my life, they are always there for me; in fact, by virtue of their professions, as attentive lawyers, they are always there for many, many people in our community.

My three beautiful girls...

Carrie, Tracey and Dollie

5. My Father-in-law, **Don Sutterfield**; what an absolutely gutsy trooper he is! After his retirement, for years, he would mow the yards of our properties and our office for a minimum price (if we paid him anything); Dollie and I are so immensely proud of him, he shows his love by the many quiet behind- the-scenes things that he does. He has truly been a gift from God.

6. **Tracey, Zack, Peyton, Paige and Parker**; what can I say? Zack is such a great guy; he is the father I wish I could have been! Couples have different priorities; Tracey's choice was to raise three great kids and she's succeeding! Our grandbabies, Peyton (12), Paige (11) and Parker (8), each have different God-given talents and personalities and are precious gifts of love for Dollie and I to treasure.

7. **Carrie and Doug**; both are complex people, and for the most part when they are with each other, they can go for hours without saying a word; however, put them in a small bistro with family or friends and they come out of their cocoons and generally put on a show! Dollie and I love them both very much.

8. **Zig Zigler**-on an April night in 1977, for the first time, through the encouragement of my parents (you know how parents are, they tell you how great somebody is and you just kind of poo poo it, thinking, you guys need to get a life!); but on this particular night, as the first of the PMA (Positive Mental Attitude) seminars were sweeping the country, prior to Zig stepping to the podium, there began a buzz almost like just before Michael or Lebron step on the floor.

I couldn't believe it; a buzz for a public speaker who was about to talk to an overflowing crowd at the University of Dayton Field House!!

As soon as he hit the stage, the place went wild!

For the next *seventy-seven* minutes, all he did was hold 12,000 folks in the palm of his hand; you could have heard a pin drop.

It was the first time that I had actually been told (even though I felt it, even though I thought it), it was the first time that I had ever heard someone say:

> "You can do what you want to do, be what you want to be and go where you want to go!"

> "You can get everything in life that you want, if you *just help enough other people get what they want!*"

> "It's your attitude, not your aptitude, that will ultimately determine your altitude in life."

> "But you've got to have goals; you've got to have a blueprint for your life; you can't be a *wondering generality*; you must be a <u>meaningful specific</u>!

> "That you can't shoot with a shotgun; you've got to aim with a rifle!

Zig, that night, became my mentor, my hero and all the things embellished in one philosophy that I wanted to be!

9. **Oscar Robertson**-I have already shared with you how Oscar, unknowingly, had such a positive influence in my life.

I had the occasion a few years ago to share with Oscar how much of his life, his presence meant to me; he was very kind as he listened to my story.

He seemed genuinely touched.

10. **Sally Curtis**; as I transferred from Leesburg-Fairfield to Martinsville High School (you'll remember that was the "longest summer ever!").   I made a presumption that it would be just as easy to "take out" teachers in this new school as it had been my mission in Leesburg.

Thus, the first day of my sophomore English class, there was this little lady named Mrs. Curtis; now Mrs. Curtis could not have weighed over 108 pounds, soaking wet, and I made it my goal that she would be the first person that we would drive crazy; that we would drive her to "drink heavily" within the first three or four weeks.

Thinking I would kind of weigh the situation through before I made my moves, I thought perhaps within 8 to 10 days it would be a good time to dismantle her.

Only a couple of days later, however, as I was walking down the hall I saw and overheard Mrs. Curtis saying to Gary, a popular high school senior, in a very strong voice, "*and another thing* Mister, if you ever do that in this class again, you will be more than *just sorry*! Do you understand?"

Wow, *this cat* was the best physically defined human being for a senior in high school I had ever seen! Gary had been shaving since sixth grade, had muscles of a body builder and I knew if she was able to take care of Gary Wheeler, that Butch Peelle would never be a match!

Later, when I was teaching at the old Wilmington Jr. High School, Sally Curtis and I became very close friends. It's interesting that teachers are real people with real needs, are very sensitive and for many of them, there is a different side in the teacher's lounge than there is in the classroom.

I always loved and respected how Sally Curtis handled her classes, how she was a loving Mother to her three children and a very highly respected member of the Clinton County area community.

11. **Esther Williams**, one of the most formidable educators in the last half century in Wilmington, Ohio.

At the time I was introduced to Esther, I was one of those seniors bused from Martinsville into the big city, thrown into an English class room with the brightest kids in the senior class; I had a very limited vocabulary combined with an even lesser desire to understand dangling participles.

Later after high school she allowed me to become close to her (which was a gift since she was a very private person).

Over the next years, she followed my progress and would often call to continue her encouragement.

I wish she was still here so that she could edit this book; it would be better because of her gifted touch.

12. **Stanley Kellough** touched my life in many different ways; early on, as a High School senior, he was my math teacher for Algebra II and a pre-calculus course.

Mr. Kellough had entered the real estate profession several years before he retired from the classroom; he was one of the few part time realtors to ever reach a strong level of success as a "part timer"; once he entered the real estate business full-time, he was unbelievable; his level of integrity, character and honesty were never questioned.

Years later, it was always a pleasure to pop in and visit him; he was one of the brightest, most clever conversationalist that I have ever had the pleasure of knowing; a superb individual, who during his time in our community made Wilmington, Ohio a much better place.

13. In the center row at the bottom is **J. Meredith Darbyshire**; after fifteen months at the Bailey-Murphy Company, I had the opportunity to join the number one office, Darbyshire and Associates, Inc.

Mr. Darbyshire was known for his hard driving style; through he and his attorney, Fred Buckley, whose office happened to be right across the street, I learned a great deal by observing how these two professionals conducted their business activities.

Sometimes, Darby would dictate a purchase agreement to Marge, six or eight or ten times before he got it exactly the way he wanted it.

He was bright, he was gifted; he was a very capable businessman.

It's interesting; he told me more than once, how when he first got into the real estate business, the first two years he knocked on every door in the Sabina area; he got up on the back of the tractor or combine of nearly every farmer in Clinton County and said, "Hey, if there's ever a time that you might want to sell your farm or know anybody that might want to, give old Darby a call."

Darby, also *"did what the failures are afraid to do!"*

14.   **Tom Hopkins**, perhaps the greatest real estate residential sales trainer in the country! One of my favorite serious Tommy Hopkins story (he has so many great, funny things that have occurred to him as a real estate salesperson; he'll keep you rolling with his humorous and crazy stories). But this one went straight to my heart the first time I heard him speak in 1980.

After working in heavy construction for a couple of years, at the age of 20, Tommy thought there might be something easier on his body; he decided he would try real estate.

According to Tommy, no one in his family had ever attained a high level of success and had the classic "I'm not going to take a risk and lose everything" attitude.

So, at 20, shortly after entering the real estate profession, having his prospects follow him from home to home as he led them on his old motorbike, he felt like he needed to learn from the best; Tommy sought out a distinguished businessman and asked him to join him for lunch; to Tommy's surprise, the man agreed. They met at an upper scale restaurant and according to Tommy, the gentleman was very kind to him.

At the end of the meeting, Tommy asked "Is there any one particular thing you could tell me to give me the best chance towards success?" The businessman thought for a second, turned a napkin over and wrote the following words,

"*I MUST DO THE MOST PRODUCTIVE THING POSSIBLE AT EVERY GIVEN MOMENT*."

15.   Dollie and I.

● ●

YOU ARE THE SUNSHINE OF MY LIFE

There are many other pictures in my "wall of gratitude" room whose love and support and positive uplifting in my life have meant so much to me.

Within the walls of this room include pictures of myself with Jonda Towner; Nancy LaRocca, who can brighten' up any room she walks into; Terese Hamilton, Pastor Elizabeth Looney, Mary Houghtaling, Pastor Kurtis Summerville, Suzie Holmes, Kenny Hormell, Bob Schaad, Ned Thompson, Ben Kaplan, Ken Hawk, Tommy Donaldson, Shawn Long, Derek Miller, Congressman Bob McEwen and his wife Liz; Debbie McEwen (Bob's sister who I have great affection for); Jeff Frost and James Frost, twin brothers who have had remarkable success in the real estate business; Antoine and Shingi Dossa, whose faith touches me deeply every time I am near them, and Pam Stricker (publisher of the Wilmington News Journal) whom I have the highest regard.

Also, the Michael and Saundra Juniet family, the Bruce and Vanessa McKee family; Ken Lundy who is my partner at Peelle & Lundy Realtors; Matt Williams (Matt and I originally were in the 8th grade together; he went on- I stayed a few more years); Matt has done an absolutely superb job in our office for the past twenty years; Robyn Clifton (a top producer in our office) is a combination of the energizer-bunny and Lebron James's "never give up!" get-the-heck-out-of-my-way attitude; she's been such a breath of fresh air for our firm.

Also on the wall is a very meaningful picture of Lisa Lowman taken at her closing with the seller, Suzie Holmes. Lisa Lowman, through deep-seeded faith, had prayed for many years that some day she would have a lovely home for her family. Her prayers came true that day.

And finally, Jim and Gail Walker are two angels who pray for me often. Jim and Gail are in the running for buying more residential homes than any other couple!

These are not investment properties; these are their primary homes!

There are some times when Gail just can't help herself! She sees an ad in the paper and just has to find out more about it!

How can you not love a girl like that?!

• •

Since this section is called Bits and Pieces, I just had to run this little ditty by you...

Have you ever wondered where certain "catch phrases" come from?! For example, where did: "she's a happy camper"! come from?

Where did   "It's all good!" come from?
Where did   "Wow, I was eating like it was my job!" come from?
Where did   "He's not the sharpest tool in the shed!" come from
Or "He's not the brightest bulb in the hall!"

Who first said these things that eventually scatter across the country?

For you that are old enough to remember, back in the 60's and 70's, when someone was ready to leave, they would very coolly say "later".

Now, here is for the world to know.

When I was 17, I was in the attic of Grandma Peelle's farmhouse and as I was leafing through one of her dusty, twenty-five year old English *textbooks*, a phrase popped out at me that I thought was funny. The premise was: as a kid was leaving his friend, he said, "I'll catch your act later."

For some reason, that hit me as being really cool, as one kid says to another, I'll catch your "act" later.

In other words, you've been on the stage long enough, I've caught enough of your act; I'm out of here!

The next evening as I'm leaving to drive to town, I said to my mom, "I'll catch your act later."

She looked at me kind of funny, though I'm not sure she thought it was near as cool as I did.

Later that evening as I'm leaving the group of kids I'm with, I said to the last one on the way to my car, "I'll catch your act later!"

Within the next few days, it was the phrase at Martinsville High School!

Within the next few weeks, it was the phrase throughout the county.

Within a few months, the thing had scattered across college campuses.

At some point it was shortened to "catch your act later!"

Eventually, it was "Catch ya later!"

And then, just "later".

Call me crazy, but does anybody else remember this "catch phrase" but me!?

Did I really come up with it? Or, is this just a figment of my little 17 year old fantasy brain imagination?

"LATER!!"

●●●

DO YOU ASPIRE TO BE A LEADER?

As the old adage says, be careful what you ask for; you'll probably get it!

If you pray for more responsibility, if you pray for that opportunity to go to the next level in your organization, if you pray to be the leader or CEO of your company, BE PREPARED!! BE PREPARED for CRITICISM!!

Only those who *do nothing* are exempt from criticism. Some people *aim at nothing* and hit it with *remarkable accuracy* day after day!

> *Like the little boy, whose daddy came home,*
>
> *The little boy asked him "daddy, what do you do down at the*
>
> *office?"*
>
> *His daddy said "nothin' ".*
>
> *The little boy said "how do you know when to quit??"*

No matter where your ladder takes you, the more successful you become, the more criticism you will receive; the only difference between success and failure is the *way we react to the negative situations in life.*

Winston Churchill had framed in his office the words of Abraham Lincoln: "I do the very best I can; I mean to keep going. If the end brings me out right, then what is said against me won't matter. If I'm wrong, then ten thousand angels swearing I was right won't make a difference."

....

10 "Paradoxical Commandments of Leadership"

One of the most exemplary pieces of genius I've ever had the pleasure of being exposed to was penned by Kent Keith, a Rhodes Scholar and a 22 year old Harvard graduate at the time he wrote these words...

1. People are illogical, unreasonable and self-centered.
   Love and trust them anyway.

2. If you do good, people will accuse you of selfish ulterior motives.
   Do good anyway.

3. If you are successful, you will win false friends and true enemies.
   Succeed anyway.

4. The good you do today will be forgotten tomorrow.
   Do good anyway.

5. Honesty and frankness make you vulnerable.
   Be honest and frank anyway.

6. The biggest men with the biggest ideas can be shot down by the smallest men with the smallest minds.
   Think big anyway.

7. People favor underdogs, but follow only top dogs.
   Fight for a few underdogs anyway.

8. What you spend years building may be destroyed overnight.
   Build anyway.

9. People really need help but may attack you if you do help them.
   Help people anyway.

10. Give the world the best you have and you'll get kicked in the teeth.
    Give the world the best you have anyway.

How often do you stop and say to yourself "How am I doing?"

THE ONE IN THE GLASS
(Originally titled "the Man in the Glass")

When you get what you want in the struggle for self,
And the world makes you king for a day,
Just go to the mirror and look at yourself,
And see what that person has to say.

For is it your father or mother or spouse
Whose judgment on us is passed
For the person whose courage counts most in your life,
Is the one staring back from the glass.

Some people may say you're a straight shooting chum
They call you a wonderful find,
But the one in the glass says you're only a bum
If you can't look them straight in the eye.

You're the one to please- never mind all the rest,
You're with you clear up to the end
And you've passed your most dangerous, difficult test,
If the person in the glass is your friend,

Now you may fool the whole world down the pathway of life,
It pats on your back as you pass
But your final reward will be heartbreak and tears
If you've cheated the one in the glass.

THE ULTIMATE PROFESSIONAL

Nikki has her smile. The Frost brothers have their grinding work ethic. I don't think there is anyone who can complete more tasks in a day than Jonda. Kurtis Summerville is a perfectionist, and Bobby Hooper has a never give-up way which he's played the game of life.

Doug Satterfield, contains all of the above attributes and MORE! No matter whether Doug is mitering a perfect seam, taking out 20 bags of trash left behind in an old garage, or building a 30 x 40 pole barn, he has the same *unbelievable positive attitude*!

In fact, we love Doug so much, for all the things he does (he always goes that "extra mile") that we have him featured on the side of our moving truck!

Doug Satterfield, the ultimate professional, is one of the brightest lights in our town.

When Doug Satterfield <u>looks</u> <u>into</u> <u>the</u> <u>mirror</u>, he sees a MAN.

I have mentioned that people do pray for me. Most of us pray for others as well. Recently, this message was left on my cell phone:

Hello Mr. Butch
This is Antoine Dossa calling to say 'hi' and to see how you're doing.
May God Bless you and keep you.
May God make His face to shine upon you and through you.
And may the Lord God be your guide
In Jesus' Name
Amen
Have a good night.

Bye-Bye

In this hectic world we find ourselves in, none of us take as much time as we should to touch the hearts, to visit and to pray for those who we really love and care about. It is my prayer that you and I will be more like my friend, Antoine Dossa.

I SAY A LITTLE PRAYER

I believe it's a series of little things that we do on a day to day basis that makes the big difference!

Success does not come crashing down like a torrential downpour; rather, it comes slowly, one drop at a time.

Currently, I just happen to have a little prayer that I see when I open up my top dresser drawer in the morning as well as in the evening. It's a simple prayer:

Please, Father,
tell me
what to do.
        Love, Butch

It's there, where I see it at least twice a day, to remind me that I always need to be <u>listening</u> <u>to</u> <u>Him</u>.

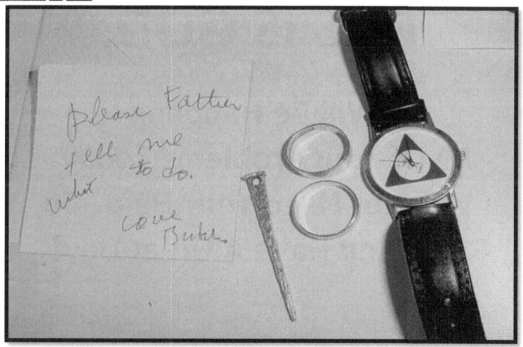

MANY PEOPLE WHO HAVE LIFTED THEMSELVES UP TO
GO ON TO OBTAIN GREAT SUCCESS...
have left positive self talk prayers, poems, motivational pictures (all the kinds of feelings and things that you want to be!) on the bathroom mirror and even on the inside of the front door as they are busting out to **<u>BREAK</u> <u>WIDE</u> <u>OPEN</u> <u>A</u> <u>BRAND</u> <u>NEW</u> <u>DAY</u>!!**

"GOOD MORNING!

THIS IS GOD,

**I Will Be Handling
All Of Your Problems Today.
I Will Not Need Your Help. So,
Relax And Have A Great Day!"**

During his graduation ceremony in May, 1964, sitting there that night in his folded metal chair, there was not one person in that over flowing gymnasium crowd of 2,000 plus people who would have bet a nickel in the years to come that:

1. Butch Peelle would ever own a car that started every time he got in it.

2. Butch Peelle would marry the coolest girl in that high school class (may be just his opinion!)

3. Butch Peelle would graduate from a major university (or from anywhere for that matter!).

4. Become Master of a Masonic Lodge at age 25.

5. As a classroom teacher, be elected president of the Wilmington Education Association at age 26.

6. Be elected to Wilmington City Council at age 27.

7. Be honored by the local Jaycee Chapter as Outstanding Young Man of the Year, in 1974, age 28.

8. Become the youngest District Deputy Grand Master of Masons in the State of Ohio in 1974, age 28.

9. Be the commencement speaker for the Wilmington High School Graduating Class of 1977, at the age of 31.

10. Have the opportunity to be a part of a wonderful family having a lovely wife and two beautiful daughters.

11. Have a terrific Father-in-Law

12. Have two of the finest son-in-laws a father could ask for his daughters.

13. Have four of the coolest grandkids in the world!

14. Be the number one residential real estate salesperson in the Wilmington/Clinton County area for twenty six years.

15. Write a best-selling book???

ACKNOWLEDGEMENTS

God uses people.

God used Bruce McKee to encourage me to write "the book".

I would like to thank Hal and Sue Allen of Allen's Studio for their encouragement as well as permission to use their work.

I would also like to recognized the Brown Publishing Company and Pam Stricker of the Wilmington News Journal for permission to reprint articles from their publications.

And for reasons that each of these people are aware, I wish to recognize Rick Moyer, Ben Kaplan, John Chambers, Jeff Cloud, Bob Wagenseller, John Limbert, Jack Powell, Michael Graham, R.A. Williams, Ron Shidaker, Mark Williams, Bob Shaad, J.B. Stamper, Scott Holmer, Norma Achor, Carol Peelle, Rick Helfinstine, Mary Washburn, Dottie Grantham, Chaley Peelle-Griffith, Tommy Griffith, Kay Conner, Cindy Rudd, Marcy Hawley, Grant Peelle, Carrie Peelle, Anne Wilkinson, Peggy Hickey, Laura Dale Davis, Kelly McInerney, Pat Haley, Brenda Haley, Carlos Roberts, Rob Camp, Janet Stanforth, Heath Fetters, Buddy Phillips, David Judd, Rajiv Patel, Priscilla Meiers, Barb Kaplan, Trish Fetters, Kirk Knoblauch, Jamie Mendez, Faye Harris, Bob Morgan, Mike Rough, Ned Thompson, Sandy Wiget, Art Brooks, Derik Davis, David Howell, Carol Howell, Joann Brook, Dick Williams, Karen Williams, Melody Hilderbrant, Peggy Watters, Vanessa Haag, Valerie Begg, Susan Wedding, Janet Gick Matrka, Gary Smith, Judy Spurlock, Skip Davis, Carol Davis, Bonnie Adams, David Bailey, Laura Reinsmith, Charlie Hargrave, Nancy Moore, Jackie Lundy, Rodney Carruthers, Bev Holland, Geoffrey Phillips, Ken Houghtaling, Anita Rolfe, Patty Calhoun, Brenda Hayslip, Jody Ames, Jana Davis, Erica Davis, Joe Phillips, Claudia Whittenburg, Nancy Robinson, Ken Whittenburg, Tommy Tumbleson, Frank Shaw, Sue Shaw, David Hawley, Melissa Reeder , Saundra Caplinger, Crystal Sandells, Mike Ferguson, George Schaffer, Jennifer Beal, Jean Singleton, Mike Woodell, Karen Isbell, Cindy Moyer, Scott Streber, Lee Carey, Lois Allen, Bill Morrow,

191

Tim Rudduck, Cindy Williams, Bill Hidy, Dan Buckley, Chad Carey, Walt Rowsey, Judy Coleman, Angie Kerns, Ken Hawk, Vicki Snow, Judi Shidaker, Sandy Trusty, Eric LaMont Gregory, Brian Shidaker, Andrew McCoy, Larry Roberts, Daryl Prickett, Julie Knoblauch, Pat McCoy Romance, Roby Roberts, Roger Bennett, Ann Kelly, Bob Germann, George Phillips, Mike Dobyns, Kirby Tolliver, Jerry Stricker, David Moore, Drexanne Evers, Leslie Tekulve, Mike Ewing, Marie Jones, Dave Camp, Wanda Armstrong, Joel Schultz, Joleen Norman, James Brown, Sam Stratman, Eric Florence, Jesse Harper, Cliff Rosenberger, Patty Settlemyre, Fred Stern, Liz McEwen, Dina Tolliver, Jillian Drew Zeigler, Rhoda Alale, Joe Looney, Janet Schultz, Vi Piatt, Joel Botts and Megan Botts.

And finally, I am indebted to Melinda Miller at Fotos Etc. for the countless number of hours in assisting me for this project.

Melinda was so patient with me.

She was absolutely meticulous in every detail.

Melinda, you are amazing!

"LOVE YOU!"

"LATER!"

Made in the USA
Columbia, SC
28 May 2022

61029977R10115